Carina Becker

Lapbooks: Landeskunde englischsprachiger Länder

Praktische Hinweise und Gestaltungsvorlagen
für Klappbücher zu zentralen Lehrplanthemen

5.–9. Klasse

Carina Becker hat Lehramt an Haupt- und Realschulen mit den Fächern Englisch und Evangelische Religion studiert. Sie unterrichtet an einer kooperativen Gesamtschule, leitet dort den Fachbereich Englisch im Haupt- und Realschulbereich und ist regelmäßig als Mentorin für Lehrkräfte im Vorbereitungsdienst tätig.

Wir verwenden in unseren Werken eine genderneutrale Sprache, damit sich alle gleichermaßen angesprochen fühlen. Wenn keine neutrale Formulierung möglich ist, nennen wir die weibliche und die männliche Form. In Fällen, in denen wir aufgrund einer besseren Lesbarkeit nur ein Geschlecht nennen können, achten wir darauf, den unterschiedlichen Geschlechtsidentitäten gleichermaßen gerecht zu werden.

In diesem Werk sind nach dem MarkenG geschützte Marken und sonstige Kennzeichen für eine bessere Lesbarkeit nicht besonders kenntlich gemacht. Es kann also aus dem Fehlen eines entsprechenden Hinweises nicht geschlossen werden, dass es sich um einen freien Warennamen handelt.

1. Auflage 2025
© 2025 PERSEN Verlag, Hamburg

AAP Lehrerwelt GmbH
Veritaskai 3
21079 Hamburg
Telefon: +49 (0) 40325083-040
E-Mail: info@lehrerwelt.de
Geschäftsführung: Andrea Fischer, Sandra Saghbazarian
USt-ID: DE 173 77 61 42
Register: AG Hamburg HRB/126335
Alle Rechte vorbehalten.

Autorschaft: Carina Becker
Covergestaltung: TSA&B Werbeagentur GmbH, Hamburg
Coverillustration: Barbara Gerth
Illustrationen: Satzpunkt Ursula Ewert GmbH (Bastelvorlagen), Elisabeth Lottermoser (Faltanleitung Faltbuch)
Satz: Satzpunkt Ursula Ewert GmbH, Bayreuth
Druck und Bindung: PMLS GmbH & Co. KG, Kassel

ISBN/Bestellnummer: 978-3-403-20873-0
www.persen.de

Was ist ein Lapbook?

Ein Lapbook ist ein aus Papier gestaltetes Klapp-buch oder Klappplakat zum Präsentieren von Lerninhalten. Beim Aufklappen des Plakates sollen die Lerninhalte durch unterschiedliche Elemente, z. B. Bilder, Drehscheiben, kleine Ta-schen usw., ansprechend gestaltet werden. Die verschiedenen Elemente werden in das Lapbook geklebt oder geheftet.

Das individuelle Ausgestalten der Faltkörper bie-tet den Schülerinnen und Schülern die Möglich-keit, sich kreativ und selbstständig mit den be-handelten Inhalten auseinanderzusetzen. Aus der Arbeit mit den Lapbooks resultiert immer ein eigenes, selbst hergestelltes Produkt, sodass es keine allgemeingültige Lösung gibt.

Zielsetzung

Die Schülerinnen und Schüler
* setzen sich intensiv mit dem aktuellen Thema auseinander,
* verschaffen sich selbstständig Informationen,
* arbeiten individuell,
* dokumentieren und präsentieren ihre Ergeb-nisse,
* lernen und wiederholen Inhalte (z. B. für eine Klassenarbeit).

Einsatz im Unterricht

Vor Beginn der Arbeit müssen die inhaltlichen Schwerpunkte festgelegt werden.

Die Gestaltung von Lapbooks fördert Kompeten-zen wie Selbstständigkeit, Kreativität, Kommuni-kation und stärkt die Fachkompetenz in den je-weiligen Lerninhalten.

Ein Lapbook kann in verschiedenen Sozialfor-men wie Einzelarbeit, Partnerarbeit oder Grup-penarbeit erstellt werden. Auch leistungsschwä-chere Schülerinnen und Schüler bekommen so die Möglichkeit, ihre Stärken einzubringen. Für sie wäre es zudem ideal, als Hilfestellung einen „Lageplan" für die einzelnen Klappelemente und die Gestaltung des Lapbooks anzubieten.

Je nach Leistungsstand und der zur Verfügung stehenden Bearbeitungszeit können den Schüle-rinnen und Schülern inhaltlich abgestimmte Ar-beitsaufträge und Faltvorlagen angeboten wer-den.

Bei der Einführung ist es auch möglich, der Lern-gruppe ein fertig gebasteltes Lapbook als Vorla-ge bereitzustellen, um den Entstehungsprozess zu vereinfachen und das Endergebnis bzw. das Prinzip des Lapbooks zu visualisieren.

Einsatz in unterschiedlichen Klassenstufen

In jüngeren Jahrgängen bietet sich eine behutsa-me Heranführung an die Arbeit mit Lapbooks an. Zu Beginn jeder Stunde können die Schülerin-nen und Schüler mithilfe ihres Lapbooks die er-arbeiteten Inhalte wiederholen. Eventuell kann in jeder Stunde eine kleine Anzahl an Lapbook-Ele-menten bereitgestellt werden. Dann werden die Aufgaben Schritt für Schritt erweitert – und somit entwickelt sich das Klappbuch im Laufe einer Unterrichtseinheit. Zudem sollten in den unteren Klassen stärkere Vorgaben gemacht und kon-krete Aufgabenstellungen formuliert werden; auch die Sachinformationen müssen hier von der Lehrkraft vorgegeben werden, während diese in höheren Klassen eigenständig recherchiert wer-den können.

Je mehr die Schülerinnen und Schüler mit der Methode Lapbook vertraut sind, desto freier kön-nen sie sich ein Thema erarbeiten, bis sie irgend-wann nur noch Blankovorlagen erhalten und sich dem Thema ganz eigenständig widmen können.

Material

Zur Herstellung von Lapbooks sollten folgende Materialien zur Verfügung stehen:
* DIN-A3-Plakate (Tonkarton)
* Faltvorlagen
* Musterbeutelklammern
* Scheren
* Kleber
* verschiedene Stifte

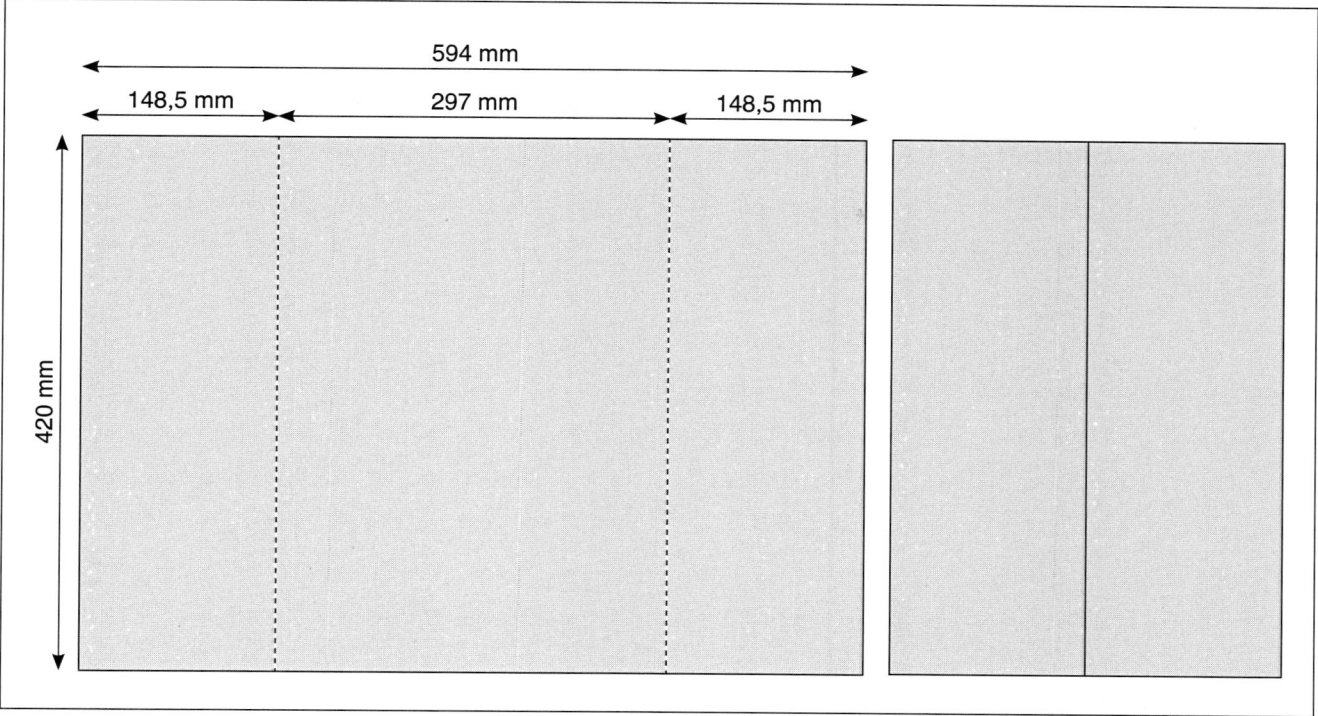

Herstellung eines Lapbooks

Das DIN-A3-Plakat kann folgendermaßen zu einem Lapbook gefaltet werden:

Die Seiten des quer gelegten DIN-A3-Plakates werden zur Mitte gefaltet, sodass ein aufklappbares „Buch" entsteht. Nach oben und unten kann diese Grundform bei Bedarf erweitert werden. Natürlich können Sie von vornherein sowohl eine andere DIN-Größe für das Plakat wählen als auch die Faltvorlagen der einzelnen Arbeitsblätter vergrößert oder verkleinert kopieren und so Ihrem Bedarf anpassen.

Das fertige Lapbook sowie ggf. das Deckblatt befüllen die Schülerinnen und Schüler mit den verschiedenen Gestaltungselementen zum jeweiligen Thema.

Die dabei verwendeten Kopiervorlagen können bei Bedarf von den Schülerinnen und Schülern farbig gestaltet werden. Ihnen wird so die Möglichkeit geboten, sich auf eine kreative Art und Weise mit dem aktuellen Unterrichtsthema auseinanderzusetzen und wichtige Aspekte zusammenzufassen.

Leistungsüberprüfung

Die Schülerinnen und Schüler erarbeiten sich die Inhalte des Themas selbstständig. Die fertigen Klappbücher können nach den Präsentationen eingesammelt und von der Lehrkraft als Portfolio genutzt werden. Es ist wichtig, mit den Schülerinnen und Schülern vor Beginn der Arbeit zu vereinbaren, ob bzw. wie die Gestaltung der Lapbooks bewertet wird.

Ich wünsche Ihnen und Ihren Schülerinnen und Schülern viel Spaß bei der Umsetzung.

Carina Becker

Great Britain and London set of clipart © Натали Осипова – stock.adobe.com

This is _____'s

lapbook.

Flag of Great Britain

Welcome to Great Britain!

What are the colours of Great Britain's flag? First colour it, then cut it out and glue it on your lapbook!

Fun fact:

The flag is also called the „Union Jack".

The crosses symbolise England, Scotland and Ireland.

Putting one flag over another – the Union Jack was born.

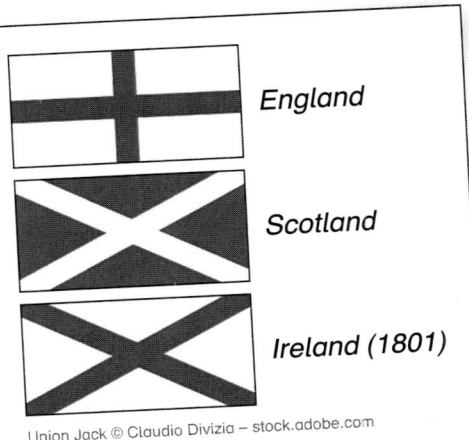

England

Scotland

Ireland (1801)

Union Jack © Claudio Divizia – stock.adobe.com

General facts about Great Britain

What do you already know about Great Britain? What does William tell us about Great Britain?

► Cut out the flip flap and fold the left side along the broken line[1] to the back. Now cut the lines on the front to the middle line, so that you can flip each fact.

► Write only short notes for each part.

► Glue the flip flap in your lapbook!

	Population
	Capital
	Language
	Landscape
	Currency[2]
	Weather

[1] broken line = *gestrichelte Linie*
[2] currency = *Währung*

Hi boys and girls,

I'm William, and I live in London, Great Britain. Great Britain is located in Europe, north west from Germany. England, Scotland and Wales form Great Britain. Adding Northern Ireland to it, it is called "The United Kindom".

Its capital is London, a beautiful old city which is known all over the world. Our national language is English – but in some parts of the country, other languages like Gaelic, Scottish etc. are spoken.

King Charles is the reigning monarch[3] since Queen Elisabeth died in September 2022 – he is the head of Great Britain's government.

Great Britain is an island and it has many different landscapes – the weather is often rainy but that doesn't matter when you visit our old historical cities and the beautiful landscape.

When you want to visit me, you have to change currency before coming here. We pay with Pound sterling (£). And be careful when you cross the street. Our cars drive on the left side of the road.

Boy in school uniform © su_cocoroe – stock.adobe.com

[3] reigning monarch = *regierender Herrscher*

A map of Great Britain

▶ Cut out the map and the snippets[4] with the parts and cities of Great Britain! Can you find the borders and their location on the map? Yes? Then draw the borders, glue the snippets on the map and glue it on your lapbook!

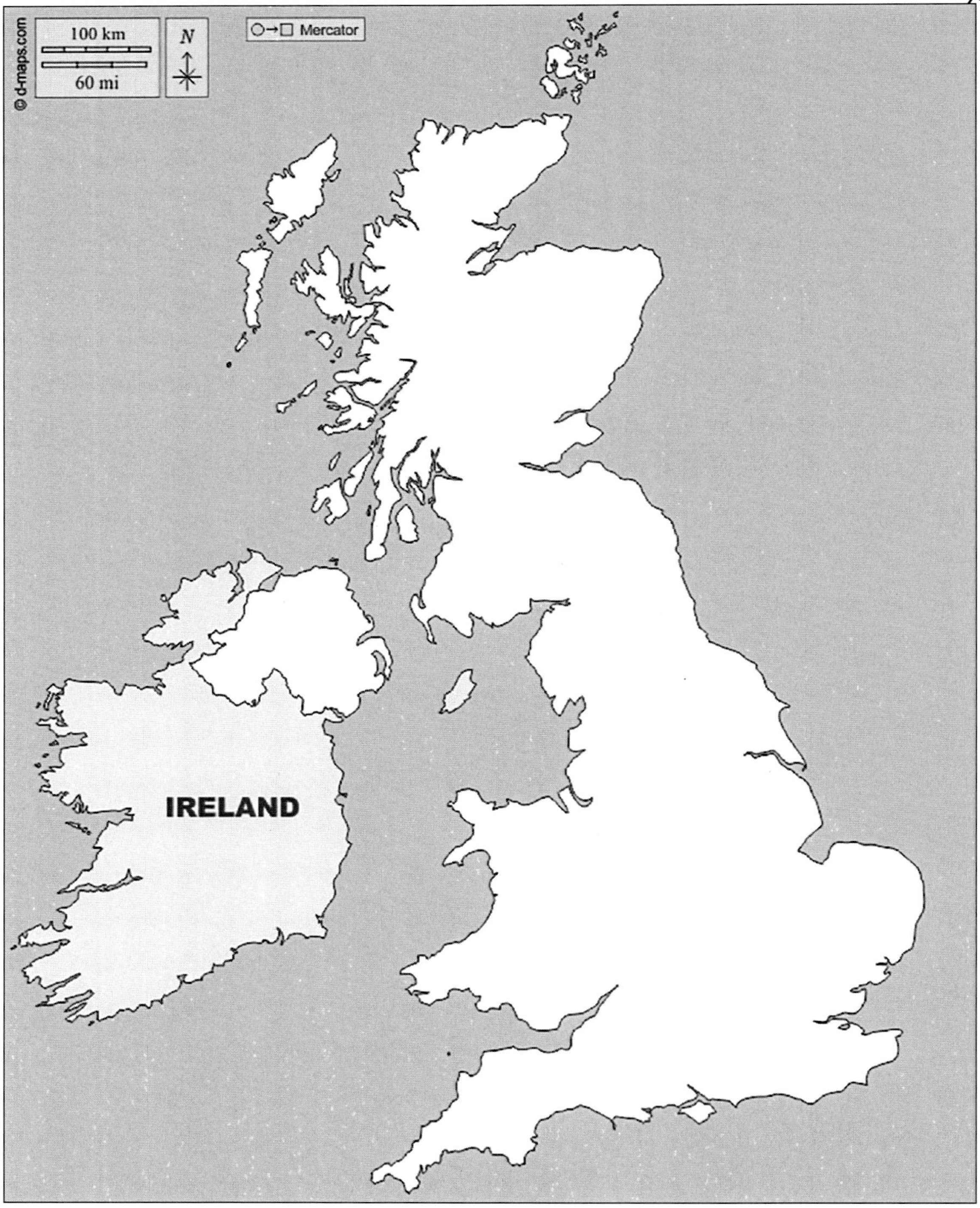

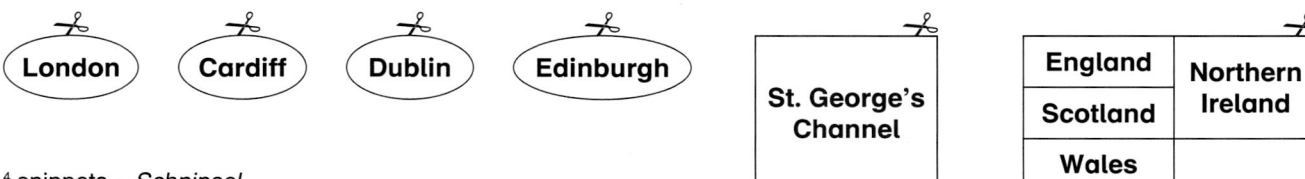

© d-maps.com
100 km
60 mi
N
○→□ Mercator
IRELAND

Karte von Großbritannien © d-maps

London | Cardiff | Dublin | Edinburgh

St. George's Channel

England	Northern Ireland
Scotland	
Wales	

[4] snippets = *Schnipsel*

Traditions and holidays

Great Britain has many traditions. Maybe you have heard about some of them?

▶ Cut out all the parts for the flip book.

▶ Find information about each flip and write a short information text about it.

▶ Glue one over another[5] and fix it on your lapbook.

Traditions and holidays

Glue here.

Guy Fawkes Night

Glue here.

St. Patrick's Day

[5] one over another =
eins über dem anderen

Glue here.

Teatime

Glue here.

English breakfast

Places to visit in Great Britain

Great Britain is worth a trip! Make a little slide show for your lapbook!

▶ Cut out the TV and glue it.

▶ Then cut out the parts for the slide show. Can you guess which text belongs to which pictures? Write the name of the places on the picture cards and glue them together so that you have a slide show in the end. Now enjoy some famous places in Great Britain!

Glue here.

Cut this out.

London is worth a trip — It is the capital of Great Britain and you can visit many sights there. You also have many cool spots for shopping and food markets.

For getting around in London you can use the red busses oder the underground.

Glue here.

When you love historical cities, then Edinburgh will be on your list! It is the capital of Scotland and it is full of Scottish charme. From here it is not far to the Highlands and Loch Ness.

Glue here.

Only stones on stones? No! Stonehenge has something magical. It was built 4000 years ago. Why is it so special?

Maybe you can find it out.

Glue here.

Not far away from London you will find Windsor Castle — it is the home of the Royal Family. It has its own chapel[6]. Maybe you have seen it on TV when some of the Royals got married? Queen Elisabeth II and her husband Prince Philip are buried[7] here.

Glue here.

The Cotswolds is a region in south west England and is also called "England's Heart". It is a beautiful landscape and everything that comes into your mind when you think about what is „typically English" you will find here. Old houses, cute little shopping streets, pubs … Come and find out for yourself!

Glue here.

The Lake District is a region and national park in North West England.

It is famous for its beautiful landscape and lakes, it covers over 900 square miles.

Since 2017 it is designated[8] a UNESCO World Heritage Site[9].

[6] chapel = *Kapelle*
[7] buried = *begraben*
[8] designated = *ausgewiesen*
[9] UNESCO World Heritage Site = *Weltkulturerbe der UNESCO*

The Royal Family

▶ Do you know the members of the Royal Family? Read the text "The Royal Family".

▶ Cut out the names of each member of the Royal Family. Cut out the sentences describing the different members of the Royal Family.

▶ Can you guess who is who? Match the right person of the Royal Family to the right fact and glue it on your lapbook.

The Royal Family

The Royal Family is well known all over the world. Queen Elisabeth, who died in 2022, was the longest reigning monarch in history. She served her country for nearly 70 years and was married to[10] Prince Philip. He died in 2021.

The new reigning monarch[11] is King Charles who was married to Diana first. They got divorced[12] in 1996 and in 1997 she died in an accident. Now he is married to his early love Camilla.

Charles and Diana have two sons: Prince William, who will be King one day when Charles has passed away[13], and Prince Harry.

Prince William is married to Princess Kate and they have three children. Prince George who will be King one day, Princess Charlotte and Prince Louis.

Prince Harry and his wife Meghan live in the USA with their two children Archie and Lilibet.

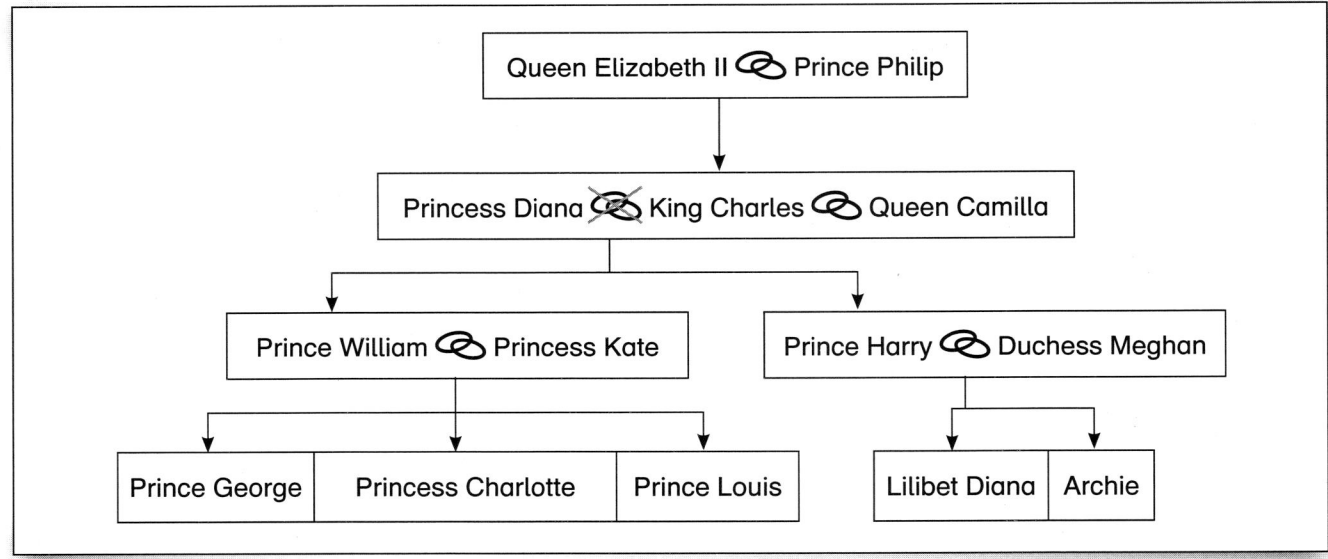

This person was the Queen from 1952 to 2022.
This person was married to Charles. She has two children.
This person is the oldest son of Charles and Diana.
This person is the king.
This person is the mother of Lilibet Diana and Archie.
This person was the husband of Queen Elizabeth II.
This person is the second wife of King Charles.
This man lives in the United States of America.

Prince Harry
King Charles
Queen Elizabeth II
Princess Diana
Prince Philip
Duchess Meghan
Queen Camilla
Prince William

[10] married to = *verheiratet mit* [11] reigning monarch = *regierender Herrscher*
[12] divorced = *geschieden* [13] to pass away = *sterben*

Greetings from Great Britain

▶ You are on a holiday in Great Britain and want to tell your family and friends about the landscape, sights and life in the United Kingdom. Choose between task a) writing a postcard or task b) writing a text message. What did you like the most and why?

a) A postcard from Great Britain

▶ You can design the front of your postcard on your own. Cut it out and glue it on your lapbook!

b) A text message from Great Britain

► Answer the questions from your friend! Cut out the illustration and glue it on your lapbook!

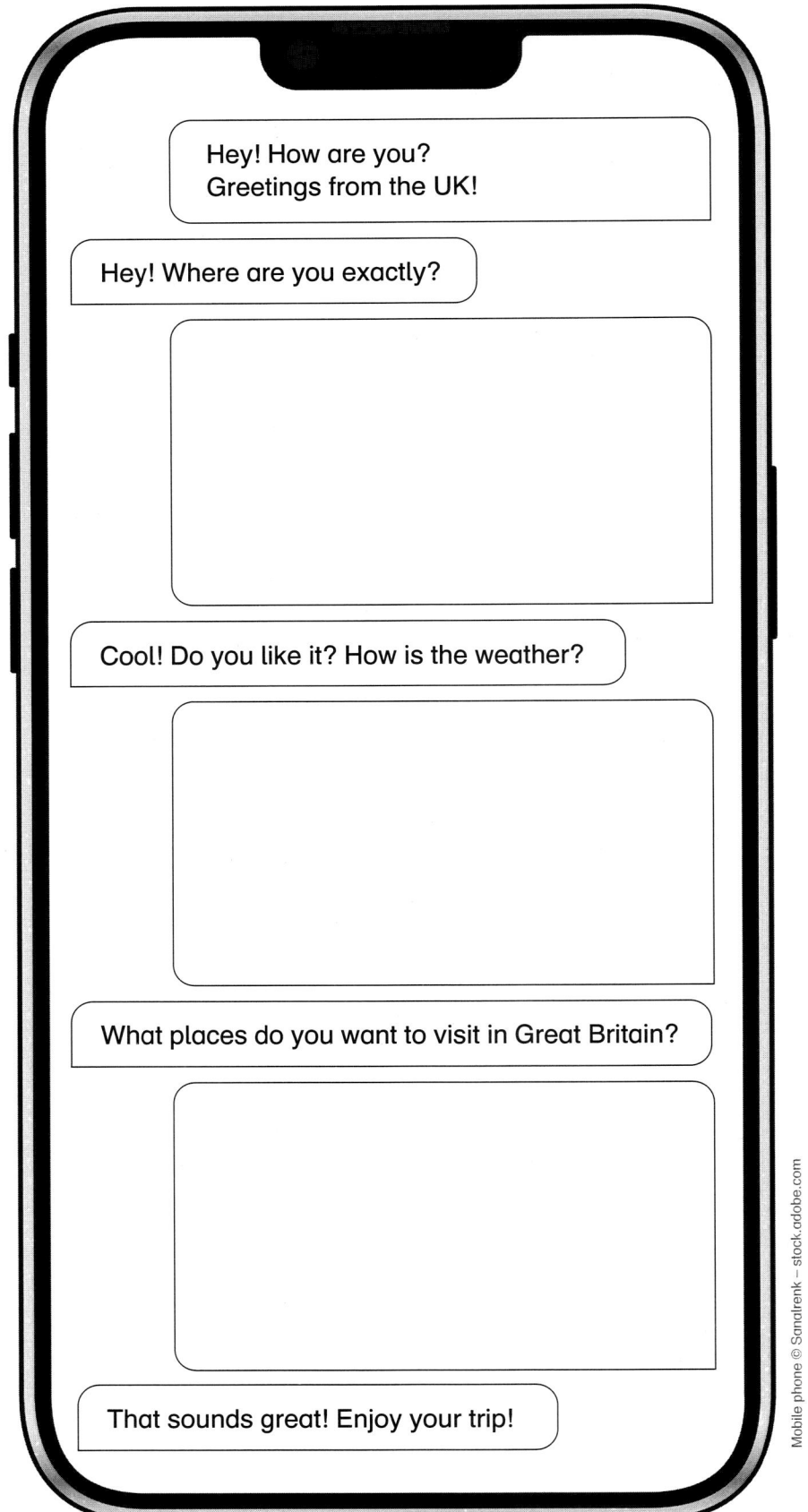

Hey! How are you?
Greetings from the UK!

Hey! Where are you exactly?

Cool! Do you like it? How is the weather?

What places do you want to visit in Great Britain?

That sounds great! Enjoy your trip!

Mobile phone © Sandtrenk – stock.adobe.com

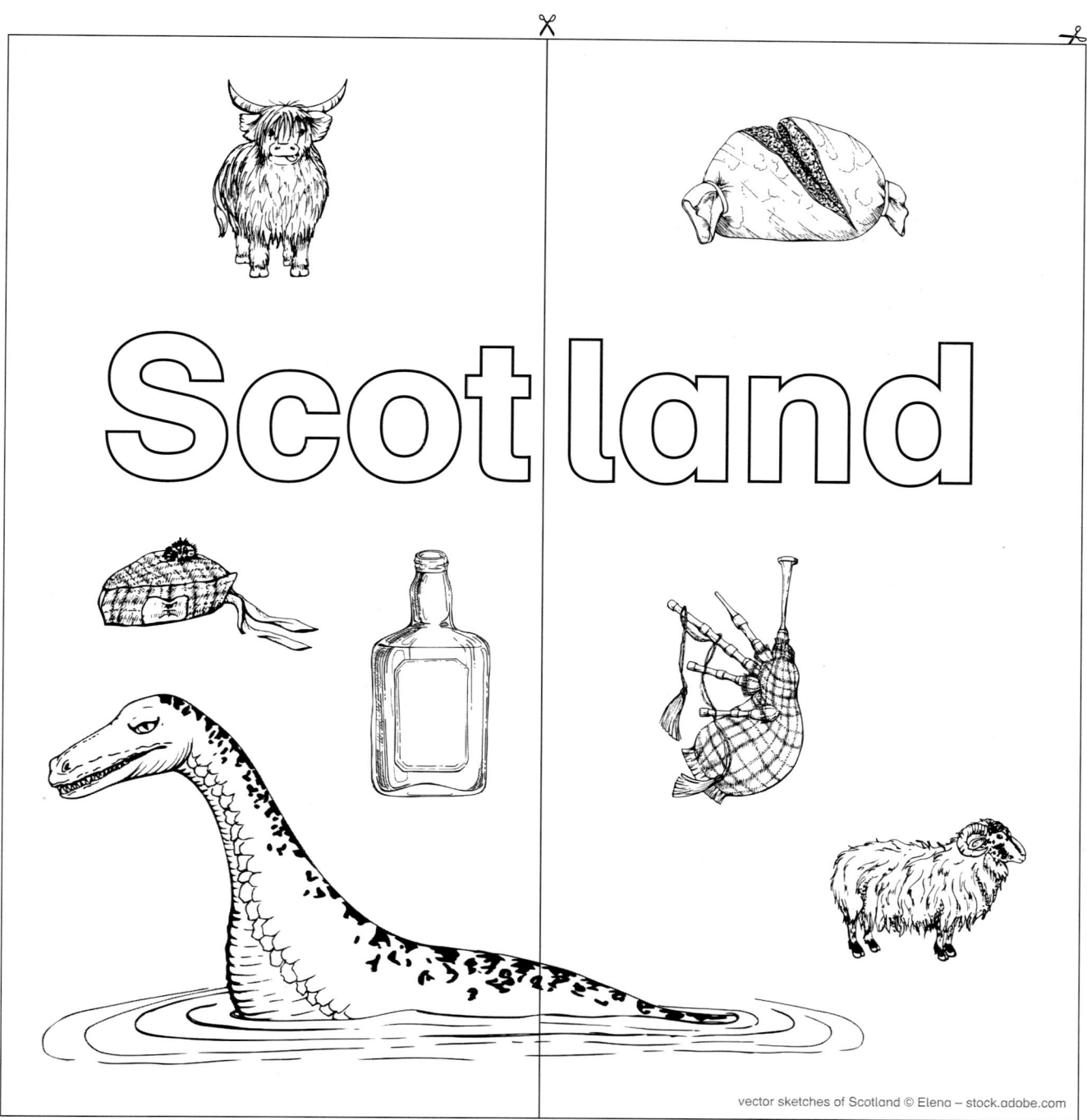

vector sketches of Scotland © Elena – stock.adobe.com

This is _____'s

lapbook.

Flag of Scotland

Welcome to Scotland!

What are the colours of the flag of Scotland? Colour it, cut it out and glue it on your lapbook!

General facts about Scotland

What do you already know about Scotland? What does Alec tell us about Scotland?

► Cut out the flip flap and fold the left side along the broken line[1] to the back.
Now cut the lines on the front to the middle line, so that you can flip each fact.

► Write only short notes for each part

► Glue the flip flap in your lapbook!

	Population
	Capital
	Language
	Landscape
	Currency[2]
	Weather

[1] broken line = *gestrichelte Linie*
[2] currency = *Währung*

Hàlo, how are ye?

I'm Alec from Scotland. Scotland is part of Great Britain and is located at the top of it. It has 5,5 mio. inhabitants that speak Gaelic and English and I speak both of them!

Its capital is Edinburgh, a beautiful old historical city at the east coast of the country. That's where I live!

With its wide and wonderful nature with cliffs, green grass and coasts, Scotland is definitely worth a trip! Trust me – it only takes 20 minutes and I can enjoy silence to calm down. The weather is mostly rainy, but in summer you can enjoy the sun at the coast and in the Highlands and at the lochs[3].

When you want to visit me, you have to change currency before going to Scotland. We pay with Pound sterling (£).

Scottish boy in traditional dress © Digital_DAlmond – stock.adobe.com

[3] loch = *See*

A map of Scotland

▶ Cut out the map and the snippets[4] with the cities, oceans and sights! Can you find out their location on the map? Yes? Then glue the snippets on the map and glue it in your lapbook!

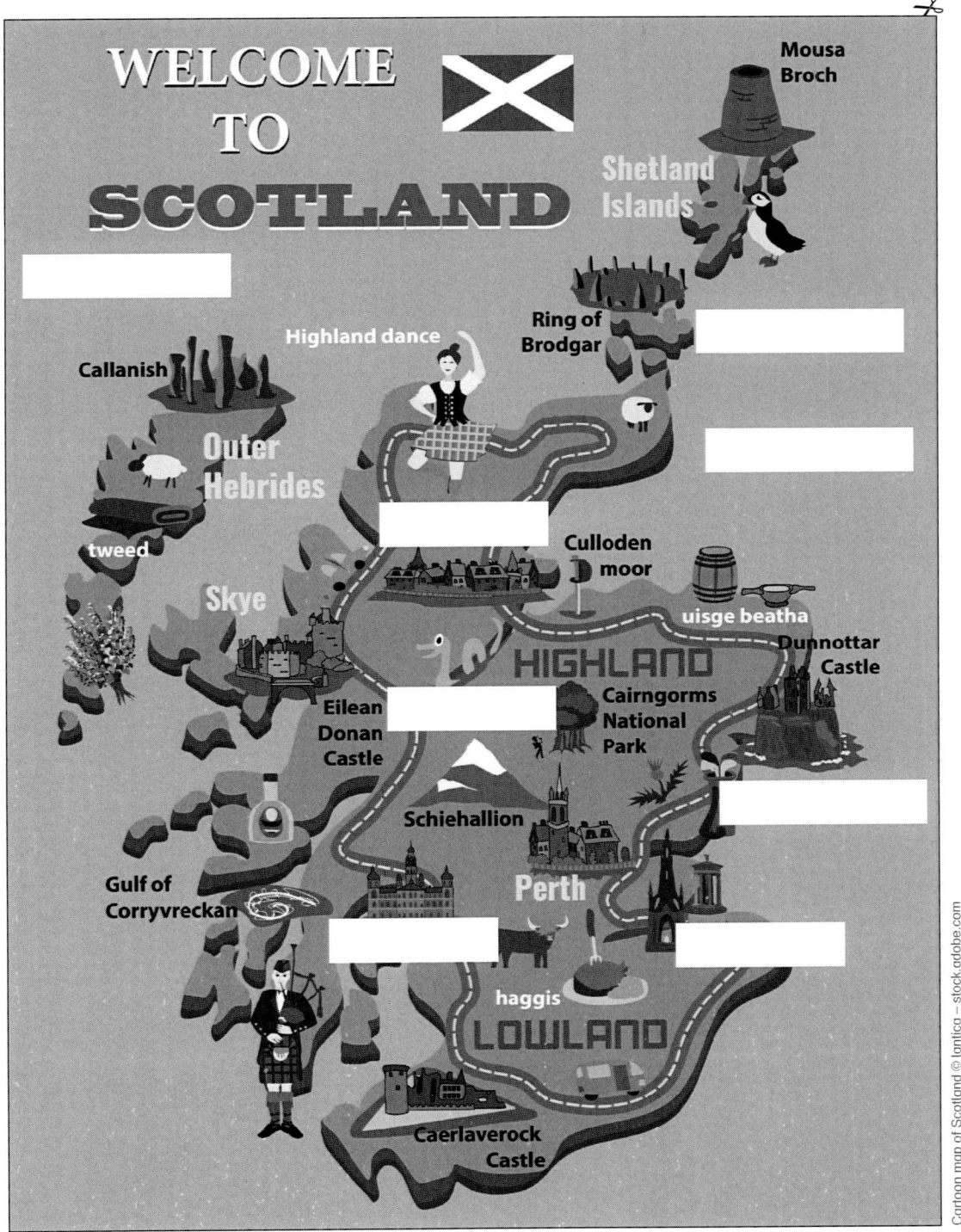

Orkney Islands	Northern Sea	Glasgow	Inverness
St. Andrews	Atlantic Ocean	Loch Ness	Edinburgh

[4] snippets = *Schnipsel*

Traditions and holidays

Scotland has many traditions. Maybe you have heard about some of them?

▶ Cut out the short texts, pictures and headlines!

▶ Then cut out the „window" from the page after the next. Glue the headline and the pictures to the outside of the window and the information text to the inside.

This instrument looks like a big bag with flutes on it. When you blow into the mouthpiece[5] it sounds like many instruments playing together.

Have you ever seen a skirt for boys and men? In Scotland it's rather common[6] for men to wear skirts. The skirt is part of traditional Scottish clothing. You can find them in different colours with check patterns[7] on it – in earlier times they showed to which clan you belonged.

Kilt

St. Andrew s Day © Vera – stock.adobe.com

Scottish bagpiper © anon – stock.adobe.com

You should try this national dish[8] when you visit Scotland. Not everyone likes it. It is like a boiled pudding with the sheep's heart, lungs, liver and different spices.

This day is celebrated on 30th November every year. Scottish people celebrate it with parades and get together with families and friends.
They commemorate[9] that he is the Scottish patron saint[10].

Haggis

---

[5] mouthpiece = *Mundstück*
[6] common = *üblich*
[7] check patterns = *Karomuster*

[8] national dish = *Nationalgericht*
[9] commemorate = *etwas oder jemandem gedenken*
[10] patron saint = *Schutzpatron*

Bagpipe

This is a typical, traditional dance in Scotland. You do it with a partner in a group to traditional Scottish music. Scottish kids learn it at school.

Highland games

Sliced Open Haggis © exclusive-design – stock.adobe.com

These games are the highlight of the year and take place all over Scotland. The origin[11] is in the Highlands. They have over 50 peculiar[12] disciplines and sport competitions like „hammer throw" or „shot put[13]".

Highlander © photosvac – stock.adobe.com

St. Andrew's day

Ceilidh Kilt

Gewichtweitwurf Highland Games © Blickfang – stock.adobe.com

[11] origin = *Ursprung*
[12] peculiar = *eigenartig*
[13] shot put = *Kugelstoßen*

Places to visit in Scotland

Scotland is worth a trip! Can you find some information on each of the best known sights of Scotland? You can use the internet or your book for help!

▶ Cut out the chips bag and glue it on your lapbook!

▶ Cut out the cards and fold them on the broken line – you can glue them together on the back. Cut out the snippets with the names of the sights and match them to the right pictures.

▶ Find some short information on each sight! Write it on the back of the cards! Make sure you answer the following questions:

- What is it?
- Where is it?
- What can you do there?
- What does it cost or is it for free?

▶ Put the "sightseeing fact cards" into your chips bag!

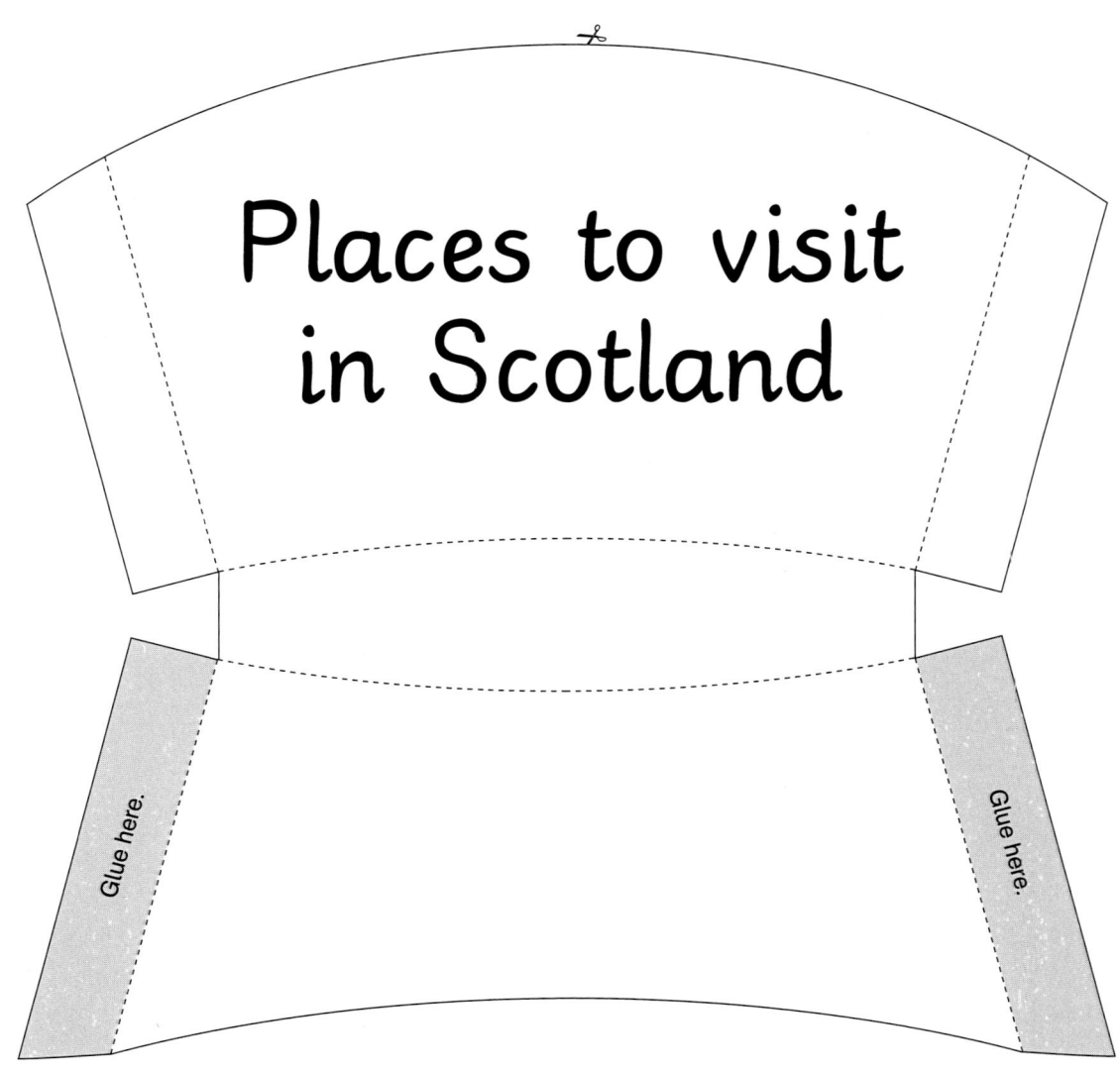

Loch Ness

Glasgow

Edinburgh

St. Andrew's

Stirling

The Highlands

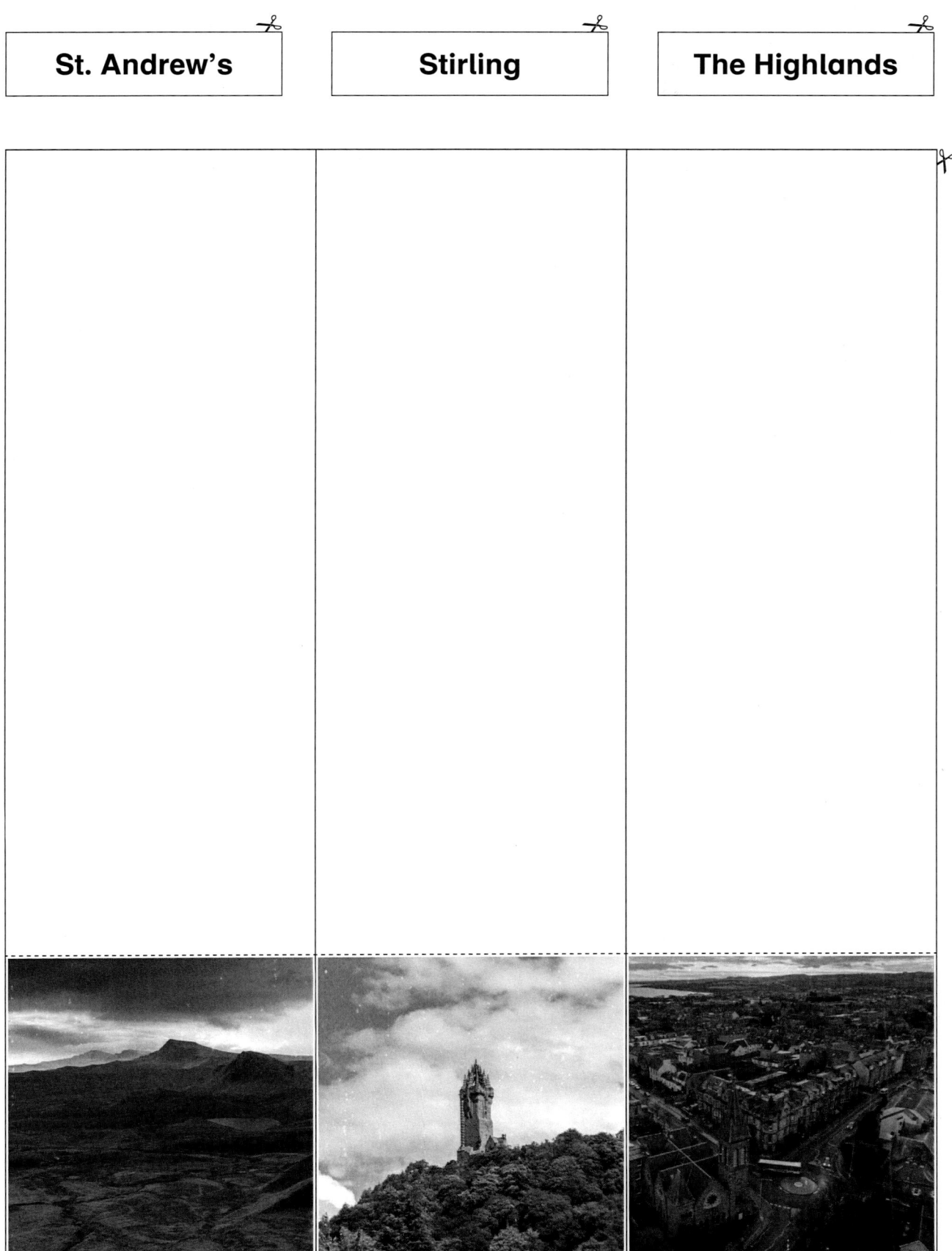

von links nach rechts: Scenic view of Scottish highlands © danmir12 – stock.adobe.com; The Wallace Monument, Stirling © Chris – stock.adobe.com; St Andrew's, Scotland © SmallWorldProduction – stock.adobe.com

Profile of a sight of your choice

▶ Choose a sight or city from Scotland and make a profile about it!

▶ Cut it out and glue it on your lapbook!

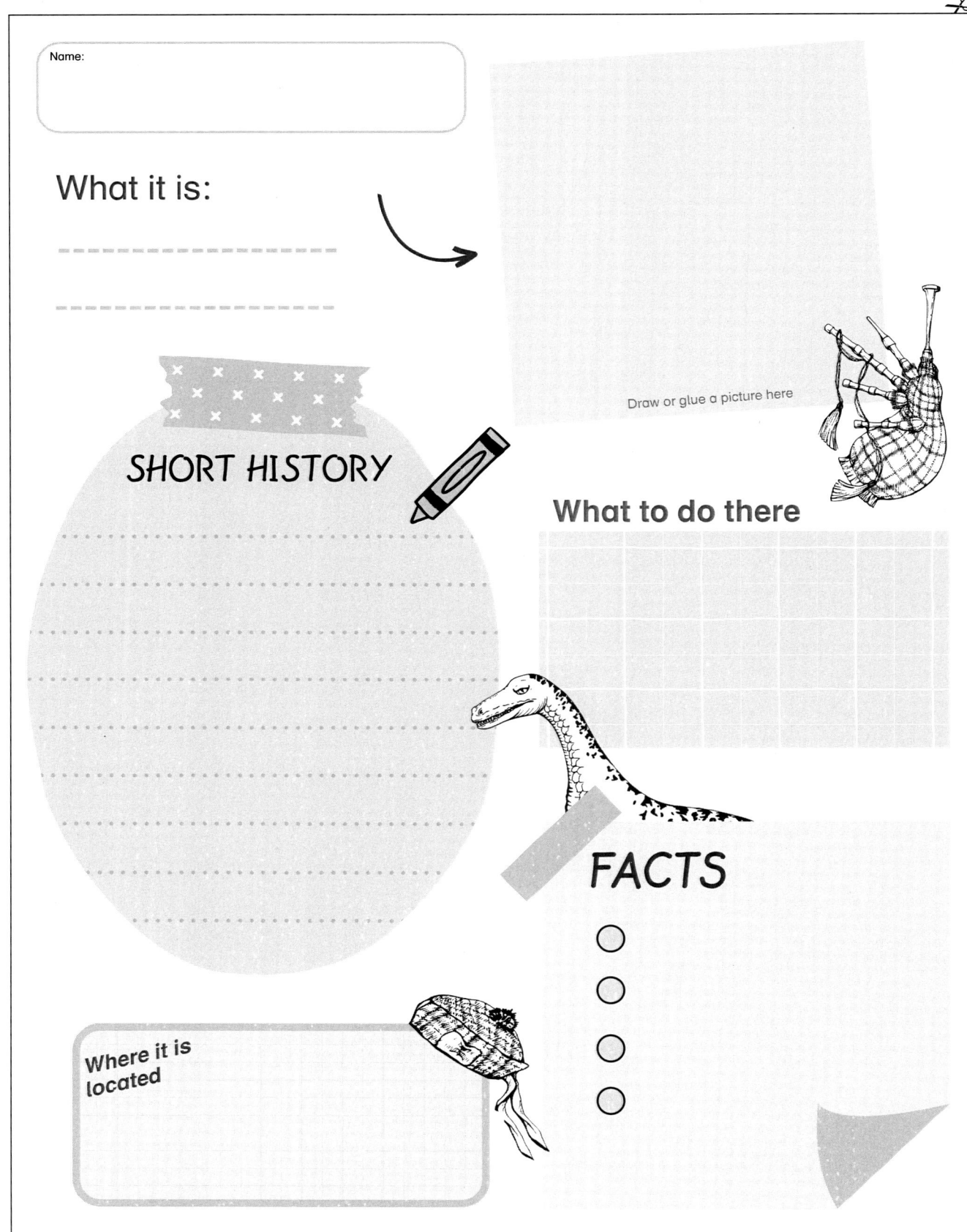

Name:

What it is:

Draw or glue a picture here

SHORT HISTORY

What to do there

FACTS

Where it is located

Languages in Scotland

▶ Scotland has different languages – one of it is Gaelic. Find out the words' meaning in English and German and write it down on the disc opposite to the Gaelic words! You have to fix[14] the disc with a pattern clip[15] on your lapbook.

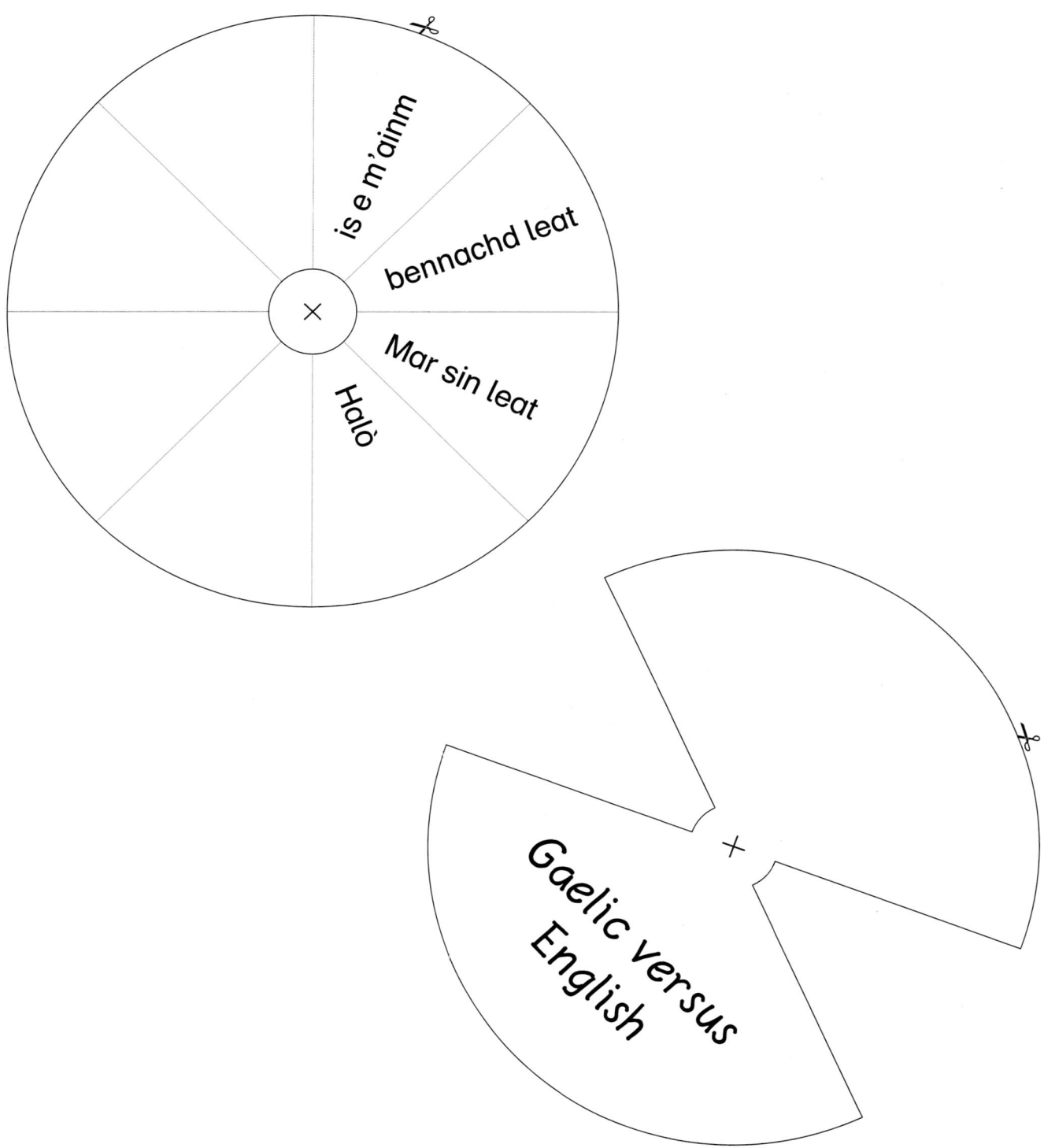

[14] to fix = *befestigen*
[15] pattern clip = *Musterklammer*

Greetings from Scotland

▶ You are on a holiday in Scotland and want to tell your family and friends about the landscape, sights and life in Scotland. Choose between task a) writing a postcard or task b) writing a text message. What did you like the most and why?

a) A postcard from Scotland

▶ You can design the front of your postcard on your own. Cut it out and glue it on your lapbook!

Glue here.

b) A text message from Scotland

▶ Answer the questions from your friend! Cut out the illustration and glue it on your lapbook!

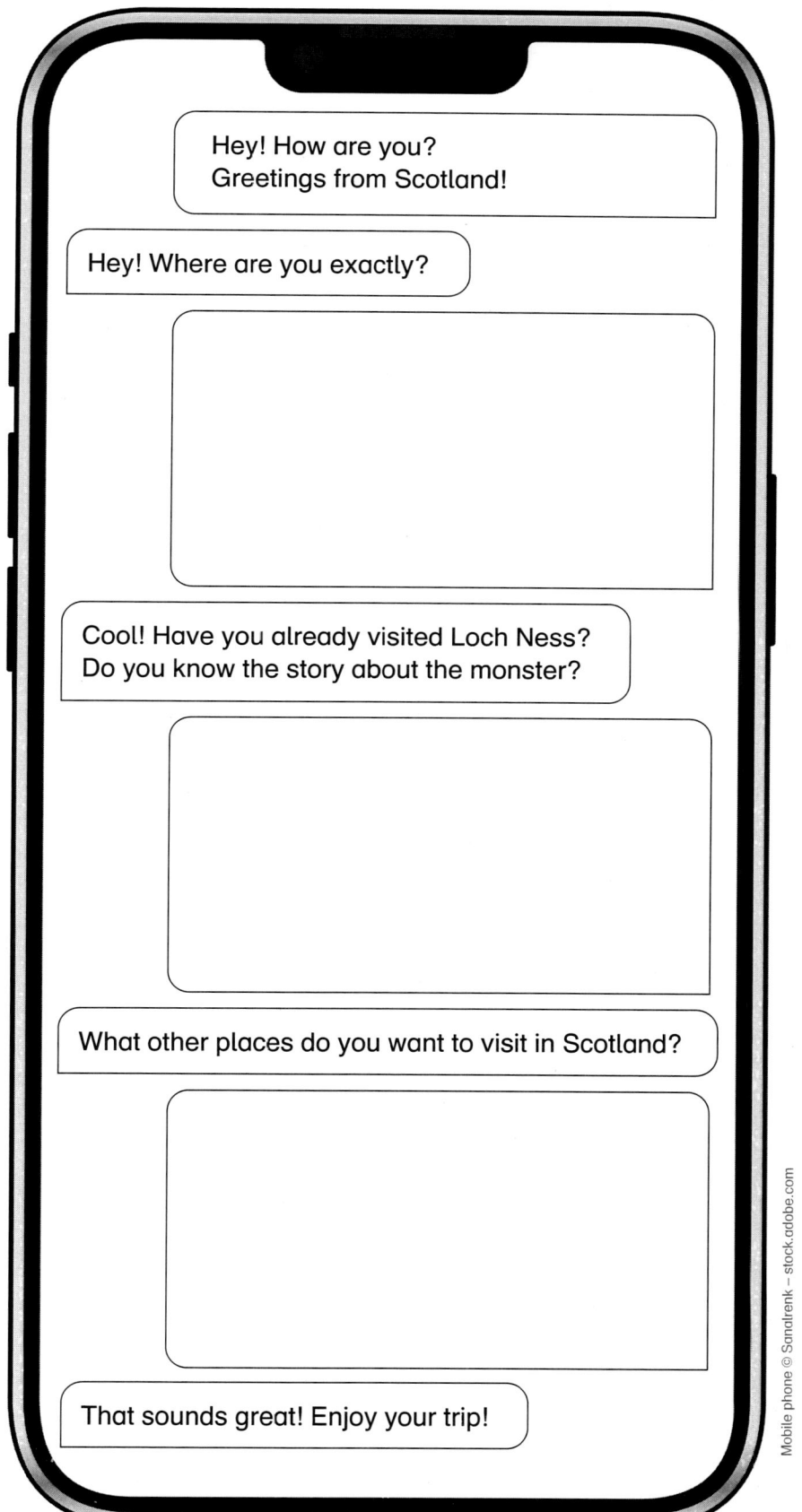

Hey! How are you?
Greetings from Scotland!

Hey! Where are you exactly?

Cool! Have you already visited Loch Ness?
Do you know the story about the monster?

What other places do you want to visit in Scotland?

That sounds great! Enjoy your trip!

Mobile phone © Sanatrenk – stock.adobe.com

Banner with the symbols of the USA © Ansty art – stock.adobe.com

This is _____'s

lapbook.

Flag of the USA

Welcome to the United States!

What are the colours of the flag of the United States of America? Colour it, cut it out and glue it on your lapbook!

Fun fact:

The flag is also called „Stars and Stripes".

The 50 stars symbolise the 50 states and the 13 stripes symbolise the colonies of the first settlers.

General facts about the USA

What does Ava tell us about the USA?

▶ Cut out the flip flap and fold the left side along the broken line[1] to the back. Now cut the lines on the front to the middle line, so that you can flip each fact.

▶ Write only short notes with the information you heard on the USA for each part.

▶ Glue the flip flap in your lapbook!

	Population
	Capital
	Language
	Landscape
	Currency[2]
	Weather

---

[1] broken line = *gestrichelte Linie*
[2] currency = *Währung*

Hey guys!

I'm Ava, and I live in El Paso, Texas. I have lived in many parts of the United States because my dad works for the US Army; that is why we had to move several times.

The USA is a huge country with 50 states and around 338.3 million people live here. Its landscape is quite diverse. There are mountains for skiing, coasts with cliffs and beaches for swimming or surfing – in some states you can see crocodiles, snakes or bears when you go for a walk, and there are forests and swampy areas, too.

There are a lot of areas where it is always sunny and hot like California and Florida, and also areas with weather conditions similar to Germany.

Many of you may think that New York is our capital because it is America's most famous city – but no, it is Washington D.C. On your map you can find it in the north east, in the District[3] of Columbia.

When you want to come and visit me, you have to change currency. We pay with US Dollars ($).

Enjoy finding out more about my country. See u!

Young girl cheerleader © sixdays – stock.adobe.com

[3] District = *Bezirk, (hier:) Verwaltungsbezirk*

A map of the USA

▶ Cut out the map and the snippets[4] with the places in the USA. Can you find their location on the map? Yes? Then glue the snippets in the right boxes on the map and glue the map on your lapbook!

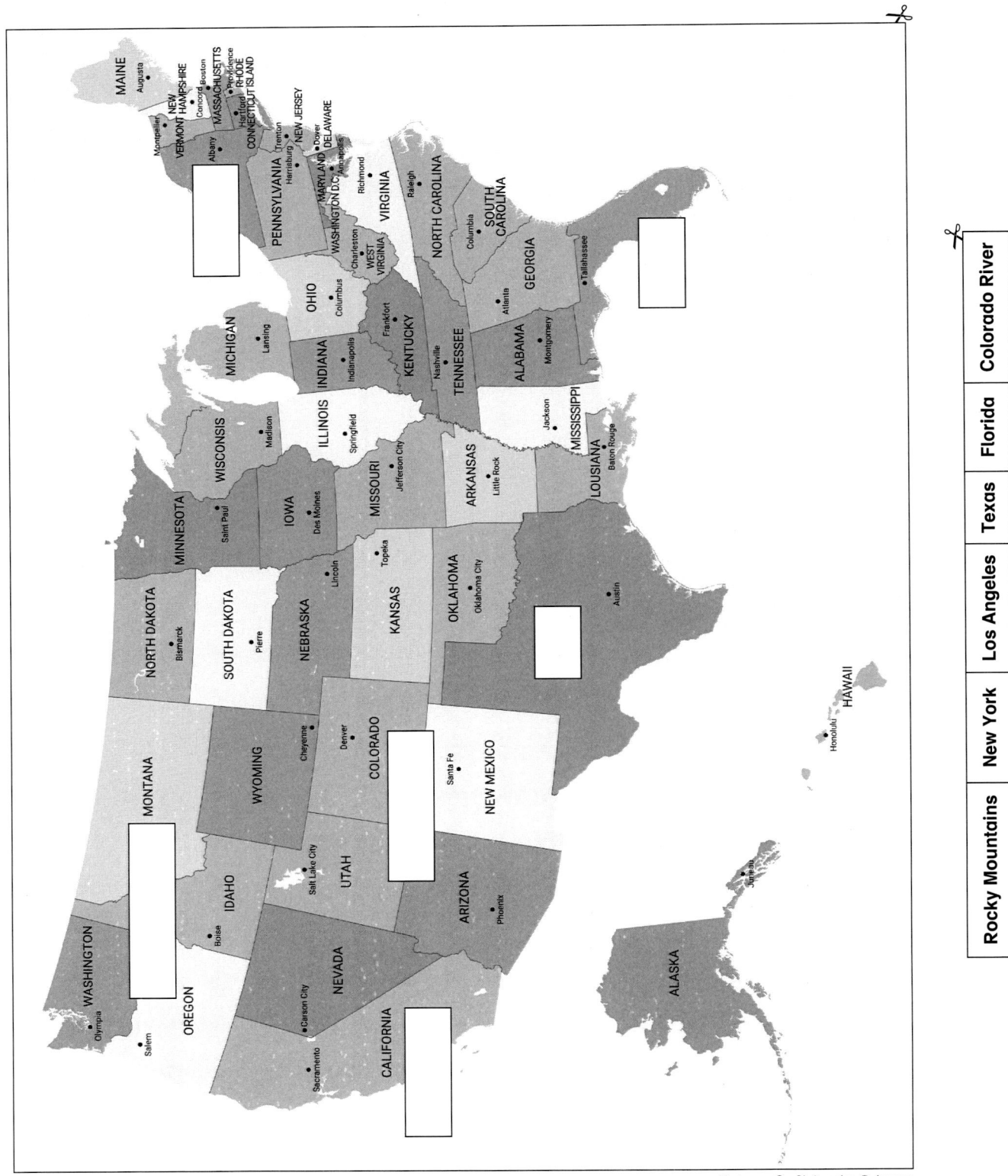

Karte von Großbritannien © d-maps

[4] snippets = *Schnipsel*

American holidays

America has many public holidays[5]. Maybe you have already heard about some of them?

▶ Cut out all the parts for the flip book.

▶ Find information for each flip and write a short information text about it.

▶ Glue them onto each other as indicated and fix them on your lapbook.

Holidays

Glue here.

Thanksgiving

Glue here.

St. Patrick's Day

[5] public holiday = *gesetzlicher Feiertag*

Glue here.

Memorial Day

Glue here.

Independence Day

Places to visit in the USA

The USA are worth a trip! Can you find some information on each of the best known sights and cities of America? You can use the internet or your book for help!

▶ Cut out the chips bag and glue it on your lapbook!

▶ Cut out the cards and fold them on the broken line – you can glue them together on the back. Cut out the snippets with the names of the sights and match them to the right pictures.

▶ Find some short information on each sight! Write it on the back of the cards! Make sure you answer the following questions:

- What is it?
- Where is it?
- What can you do there?
- What does it cost or is it for free?

▶ Put the "sightseeing fact cards" into your chips bag!

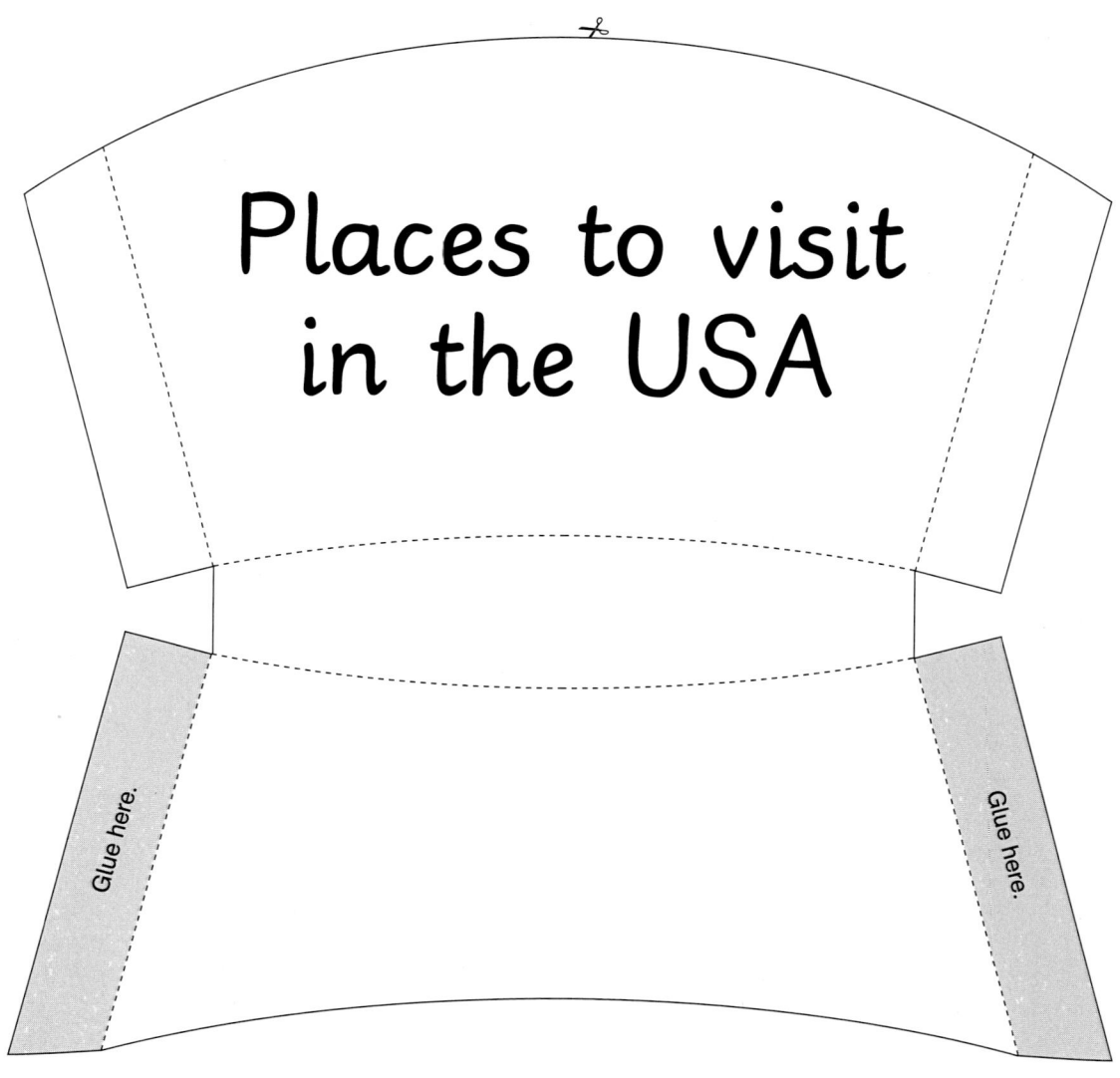

Las Vegas

New York

Grand Canyon

von links nach rechts: New York City skyline © lucky-photo – stock.adobe.com; View of the Grand Canyon © Christopher – stock.adobe.com; Las Vegas 4 © Franck Dadoune – stock.adobe.com

| White House | Everglades | Rocky Mountains |

von links nach rechts: Hiking Chief Mountain © Steven – stock.adobe.com; Washington DC, White House © Giuseppe Crimeni – stock.adobe.com; Aerial view, Everglades National Park © Juan Carlos Munoz – stock.adobe.com

Profile of a sight of your choice

▶ Choose a sight or city from the USA and make a profile about it!

▶ Cut it out and glue it on your lapbook!

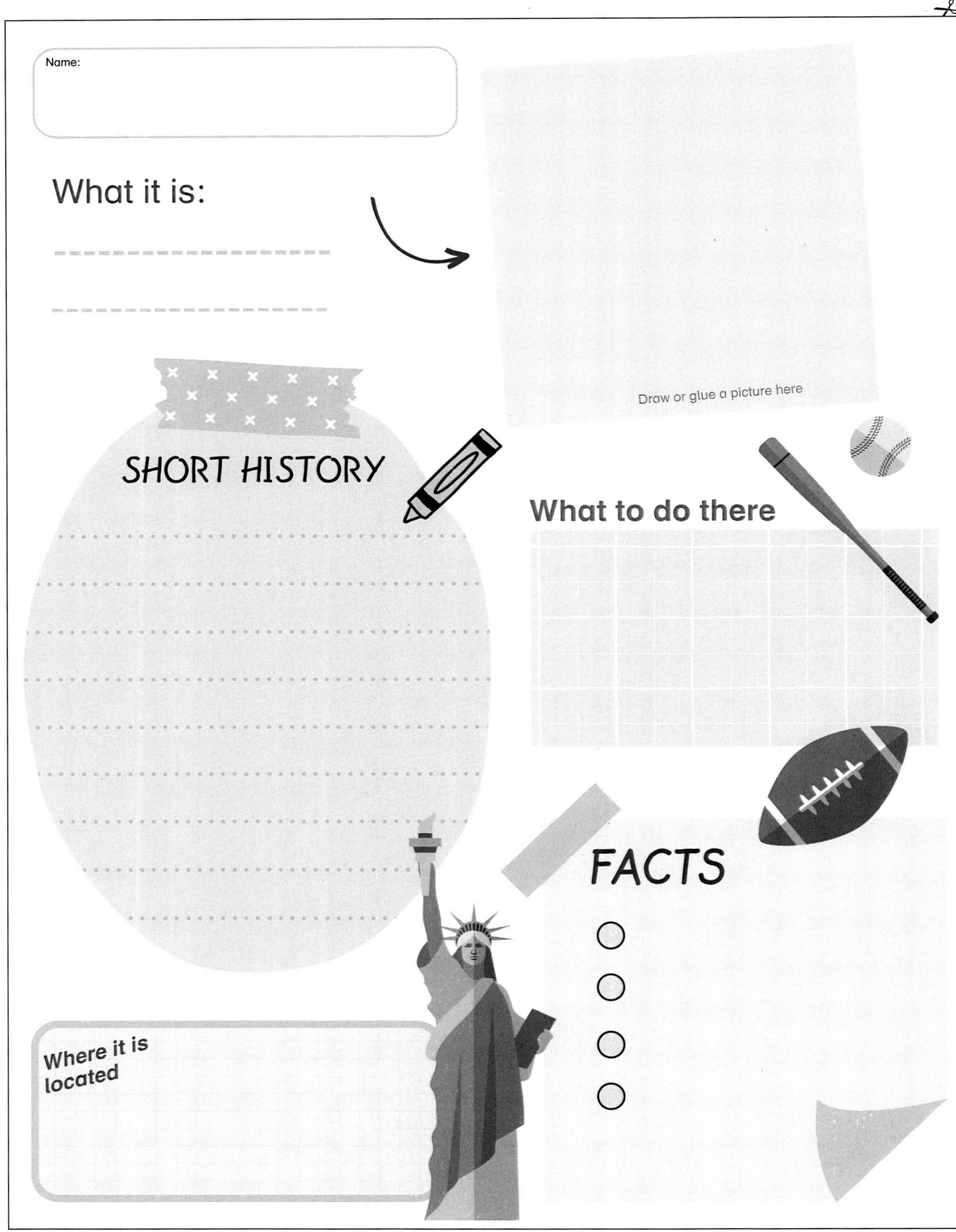

Name:

What it is:

Draw or glue a picture here

SHORT HISTORY

What to do there

FACTS

Where it is located

History of the USA

▶ Cut out the timeline and glue it on your lapbook!

▶ What happened when? Cut out the historical events and pictures, match them and glue them to the right year in the timeline. Feel free to find out more about each historical event. You can add some more information on your lapbook!

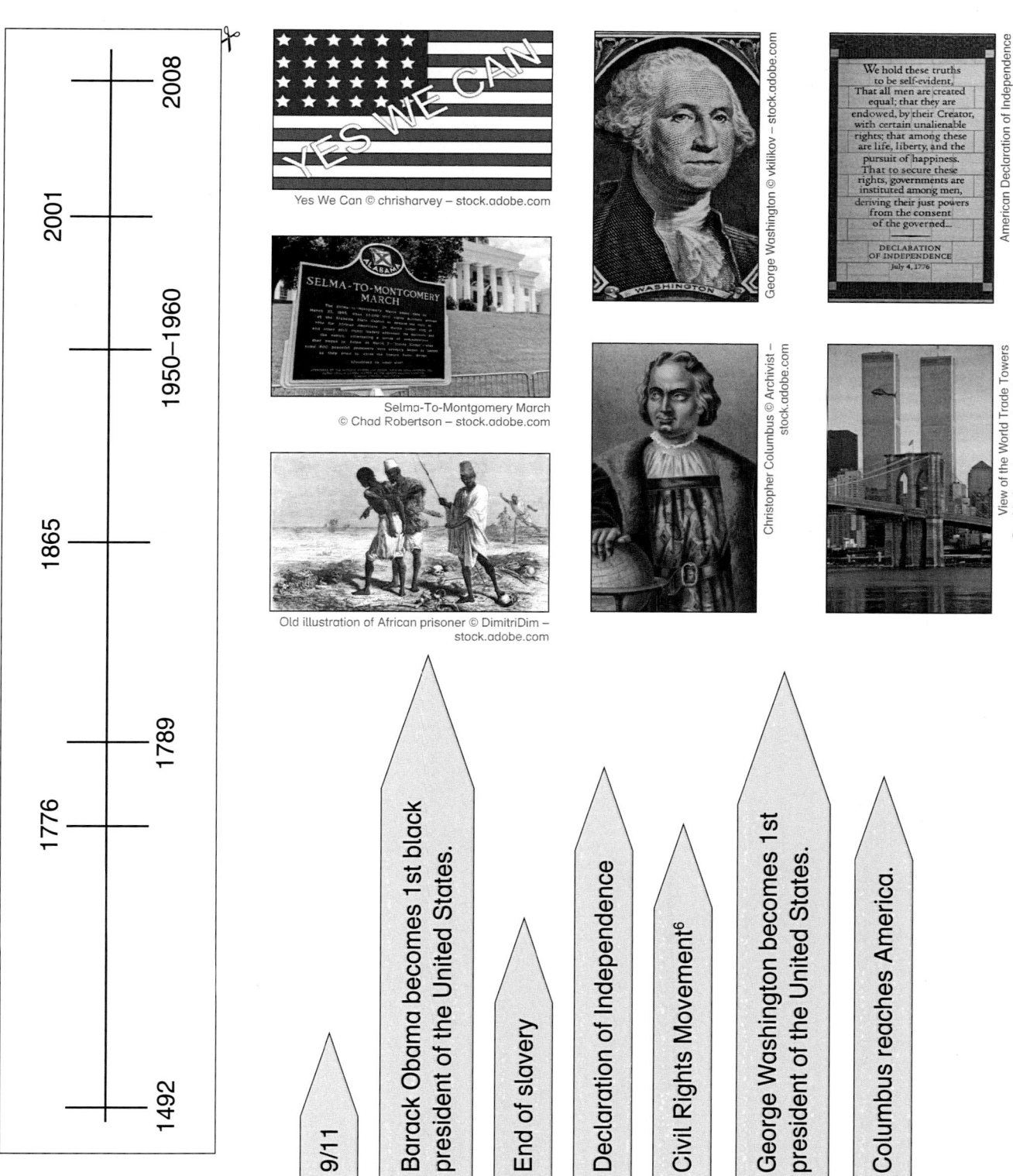

Yes We Can © chrisharvey – stock.adobe.com

Selma-To-Montgomery March
© Chad Robertson – stock.adobe.com

Old illustration of African prisoner © DimitriDim – stock.adobe.com

George Washington © vklikov – stock.adobe.com

American Declaration of Independence
© Spiroview Inc. – stock.adobe.com

Christopher Columbus © Archivist – stock.adobe.com

View of the World Trade Towers
© spiritofamerica – stock.adobe.com

Timeline years: 2008, 2001, 1950–1960, 1865, 1789, 1776, 1492

Events: 9/11 · Barack Obama becomes 1st black president of the United States. · End of slavery · Declaration of Independence · Civil Rights Movement[6] · George Washington becomes 1st president of the United States. · Columbus reaches America.

[6] Civil Rights Movement = *Bürgerrechtsbewegung*

American vs. British English

▶ Find the British and the American word for the pictures! Can you find two more examples?

▶ Write them left and right on the inside of the flips. Cut it out, fold it along the broken line and glue it on your lapbook!

French Fries © Fantastic-Stock

Home floor plan © artjafara – stock.adobe.com

Sport shoes © vladakela – stock.adobe.com

shortbread biscuits © Moving Moment – stock.adobe.com

British English

American English

Greetings from the USA

▶ You are on a holiday in the USA and want to tell your family and friends about the landscape, sights and life in the USA. Choose between task a) writing a postcard or task b) writing a text message. What did you like the most and why?

a) A postcard from the USA

▶ You can design the front of your postcard on your own. Cut it out and glue it on your lapbook!

b) A text message from the USA

▶ Answer the questions from your friend! Cut out the illustration and glue it on your lapbook!

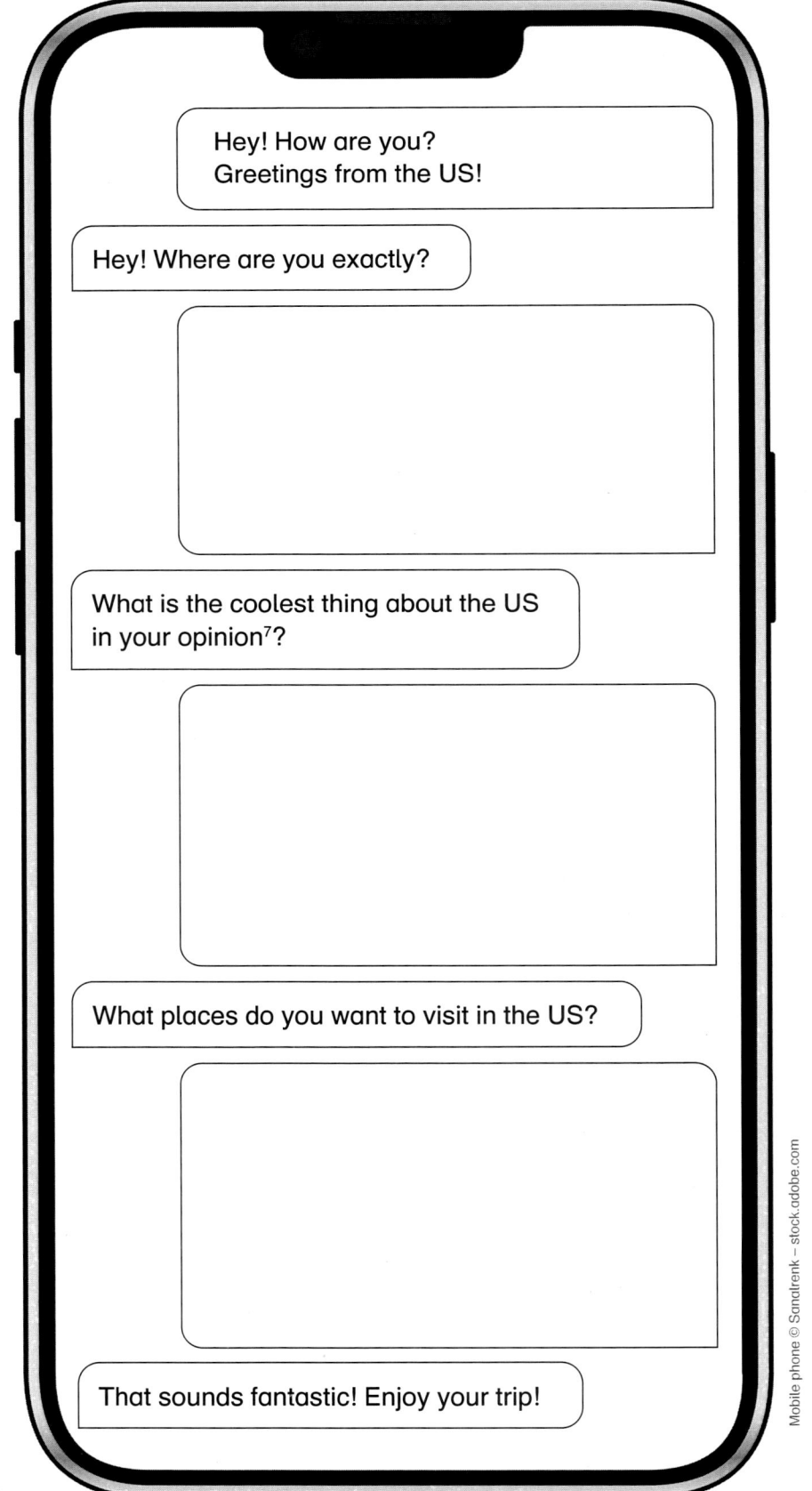

Hey! How are you?
Greetings from the US!

Hey! Where are you exactly?

What is the coolest thing about the US
in your opinion[7]?

What places do you want to visit in the US?

That sounds fantastic! Enjoy your trip!

[7] in your opinion =
deiner Meinung na

This is _____'s

lapbook.

Flag of Australia

Welcome to Australia!

What are the colours of the flag of Australia? Colour it, cut it out and glue it on your lapbook!

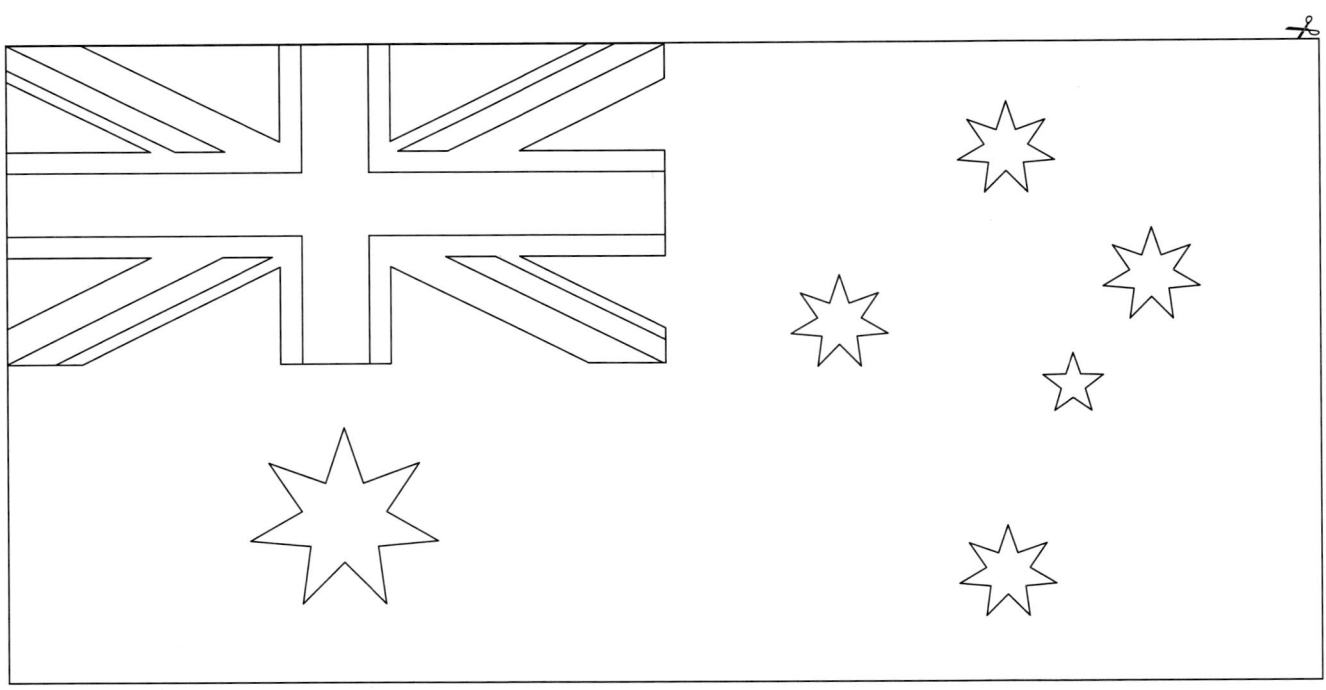

Fun fact:

The flag has the British flag on it – it has also six stars.

The biggest star has seven points. Six stars symbolise the states of Australia and the seven points of the biggest one symbolise seven territories.

The five smaller stars symbolise a constellation[1] – the Southern Cross[2].

[1] constellation = *Sternenbild*
[2] the Southern Cross = *das Kreuz des Südens*

General facts about Australia

What does Susie tell us about Australia?

▶ Cut out the flip flap and fold the left side along the broken line[3] to the back.
Now cut the lines on the front to the middle line, so that you can flip each fact.

▶ Write only short notes for each part.

▶ Glue the flip flap in your lapbook!

	Population
	Capital
	Language
	Landscape
	Currency[4]
	Weather
	Holidays

[3] broken line = *gestrichelte Linie*
[4] currency = *Währung*

G'day mates!

How are you? I am Susie and I live in Melbourne, Australia. It is located on the East Coast and I love to live next to the water. I can go to the beach whenever I want, but I can also enjoy the big city life. Australia is known for its beautiful beaches, so surfing is a big part of our culture.

In Down Under, that is Australia's nickname, the weather is always warm. Well, it is sunny and hot, also at Christmas, because when it's winter in Germany, it's summer here in Australia. Some of our cities have winter conditions in June and July. Our cities are all worth a trip – maybe you know Sydney, Melbourne or Canberra, our capital. A trip to the Outback might interest you if you wish to meet the Aboriginal Australians, the indigenous people[5] of Australia.

Nearly 25,74 million people live in Australia. We have a very special wildlife. And we have kangaroos, koalas and wombats! They are species that only live in Australia.

When you come to Australia, you have to change currency. We pay in Australian Dollar ($).

A special day for us is the Australia Day – we have barbecues with our families and friends and celebrate the first European settlers who came to Australia in 1788 to start a new life here.

Australia was once part of Great Britain, but in 1901 it became independent[6]. Nevertheless[7], we are still a member of the British Commonwealth[8]. That is why we also drive on the left side of the road!

I am sure you will love your stay in Australia!

Hoo roo!

Woman holding australia flag © Krakenimages – stock.adobe.com

---

[5] Aboriginal Australians, the indigenous people of Australia
= *indigene Australierinnen und Australier, die ersten Bewohnerinnen und Bewohner des Kontinents*
[6] independent = *unabhängig*

[7] nevertheless = *nichtsdestotrotz*
[8] British Commonwealth = *Staatengemeinschaft des Vereinigten Königreichs Großbritannien*

A map of Australia

▶ Cut out the map and the snippets[9] with the cities, states and territories[10]! Can you find their location on the map? Yes? Then glue the snippets on the map and glue it on your lapbook!

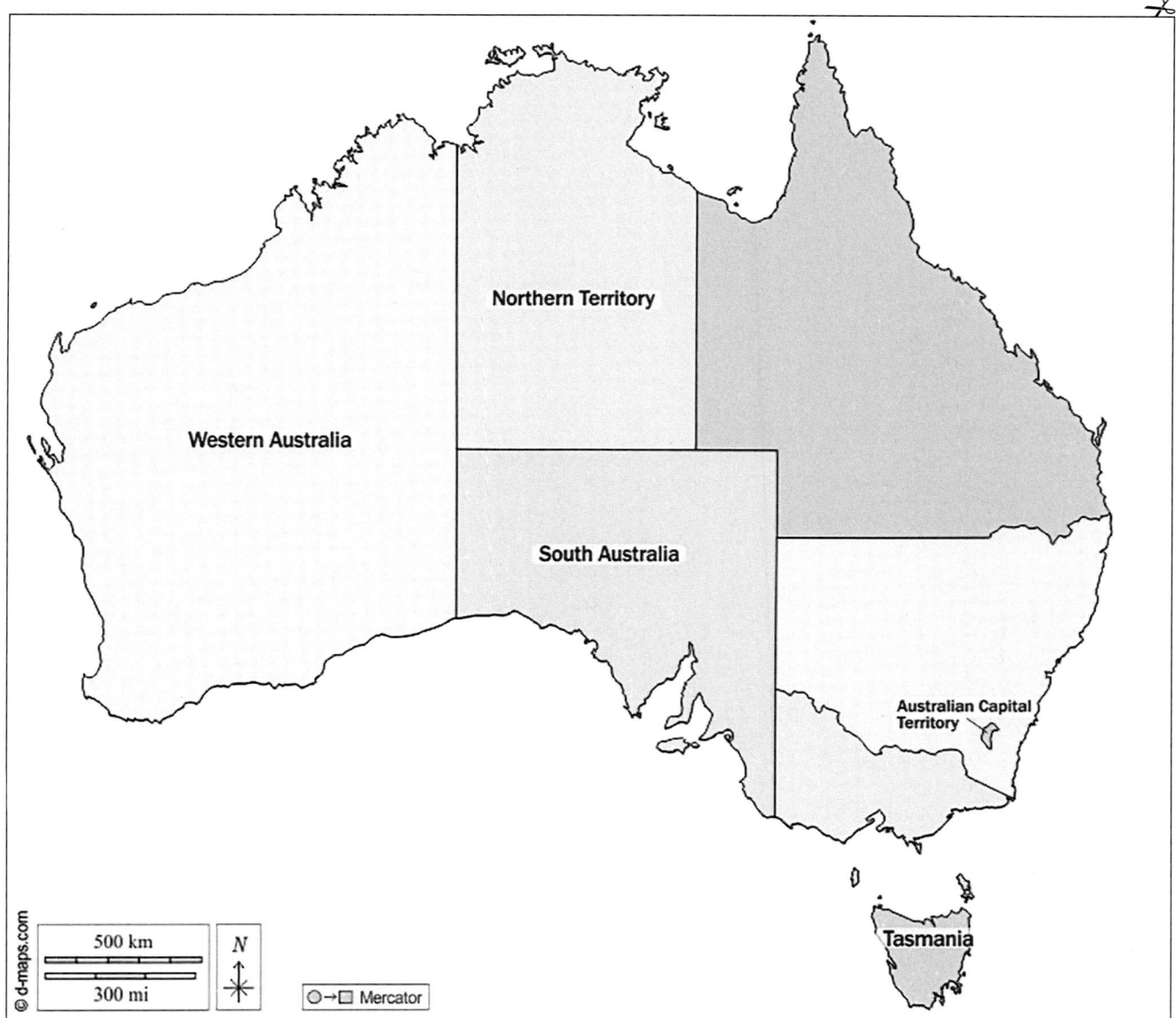

Karte von Australien © d-maps

Canberra	Sydney	Queensland
Melbourne	Victoria	New South Wales

[9] snippets = *Schnipsel*
[10] territories = *Hoheits- oder Staatsgebiete*

Aboriginal Australians

▶ Aboriginal Australians are the first inhabitans of Australia. They have a very special way of life.

▶ Can you match the pictures to the right text? Fold and design your own „mini book".
The instructions below will help you. Then cut out the pictures and glue them on the right place in your „mini book" and glue it on your lapbook! If you know some more facts about the Aboriginal Australians, you can write them on your lapbook around the „mini book".

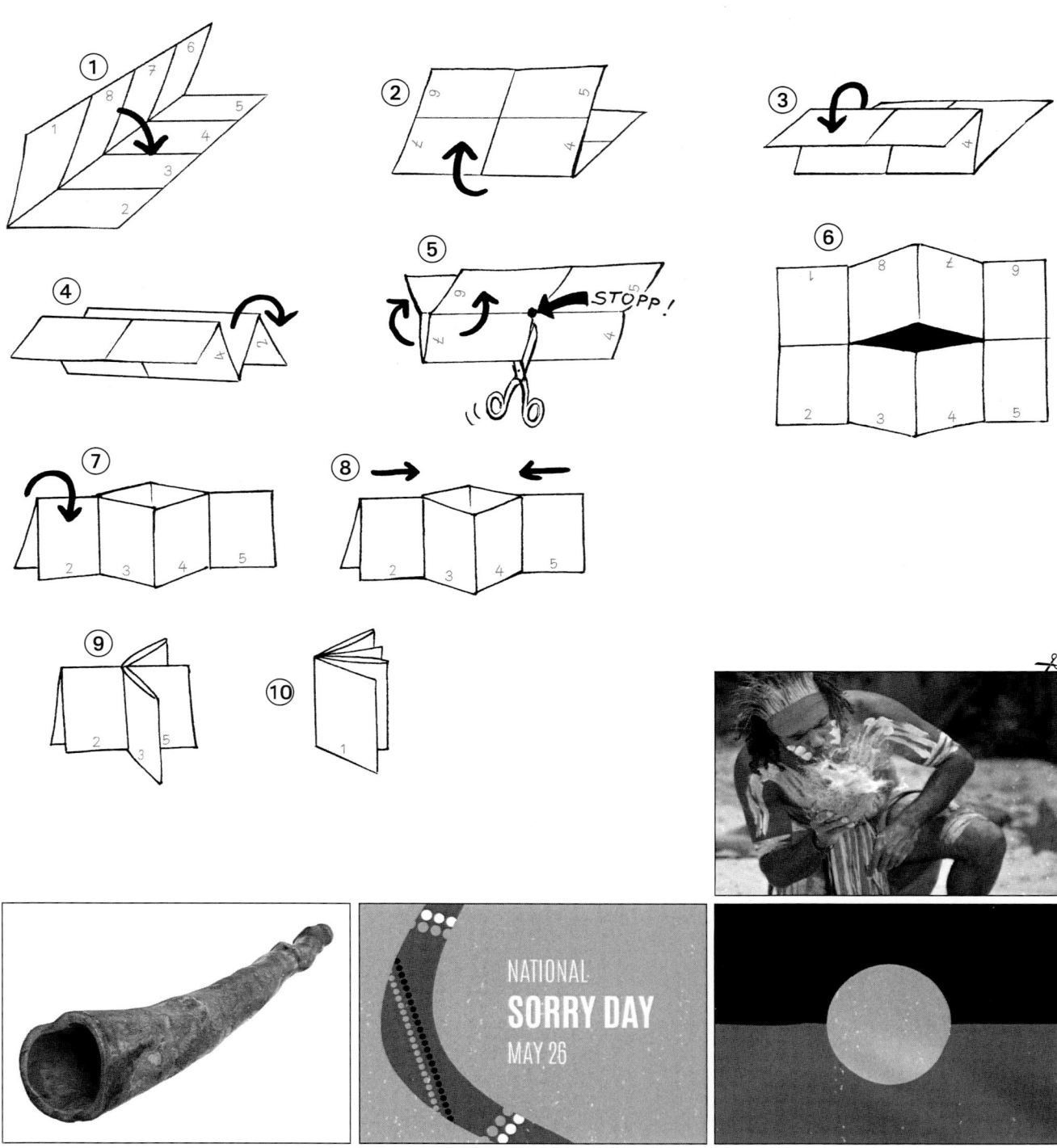

When the settlers came to Australia, they wanted the land from the Aboriginal Australians, who did not like it – but the Aboriginal Australians wanted to live in peace. In the early 1900s, children were taken away from their families to live in orphan homes and get a „white" education there. So many children could not live with their families.

From the early 1990s on, the government apologised to the Aboriginal Australians who belong to the „Stolen Generation".

A didgeridoo is an Aboriginal instrument.

It is made of a hollow branch of (mostly) eucalyptus wood. You have to breath into it – the sound comes with opening and closing your mouth and breathing circular.

Can you imagine to play this instrument?

Glue here

Aboriginal Australians are the first inhabitans of Australia.It is the oldest culture worldwide. Aboriginal Australians live in harmony with nature and they are thankful for everything they get from „Mother Earth".

Every Aboriginal tribe has its own language.

Flag of the Aboriginal Australians

Australian impressions

Australia has many beautiful places! Make a little slide show for your lapbook!

▶ Cut out the TV and glue it together and on your lapbook.

▶ Then cut out the parts for the slide show. Write the name of the places on the picture cards. Find some interesting information for each impression[11], write it on the blanco cards[12] and glue them together in the correct order so that you have a slide show in the end.

Glue here.

Cut this out.

[11] impression = *Eindruck, (hier:) Druck, Bild*
[12] blanco cards = *leere Karten*

Glue here.

Glue here.

Glue here.

Glue here.

Glue here.

von links nach rechts unten: Sydney Opera house © Marcos – stock.adobe.com; Melbourne city skyline © f11photo – stock.adobe.com; Heart Reef Whitsundays © Tanya – stock.adobe.com; Uluru (Ayer's Rock) © beau Uluru – stock.adobe.com; kangaroo crossing road sign © anankkml – stock.adobe.com; Bondi Beach in Sydney © Joseph Oropel – stock.adobe.com

Profile of a sight of your choice

▶ Choose a sight or city of Australia and make a profile about it!

▶ Cut it out and glue it on your lapbook!

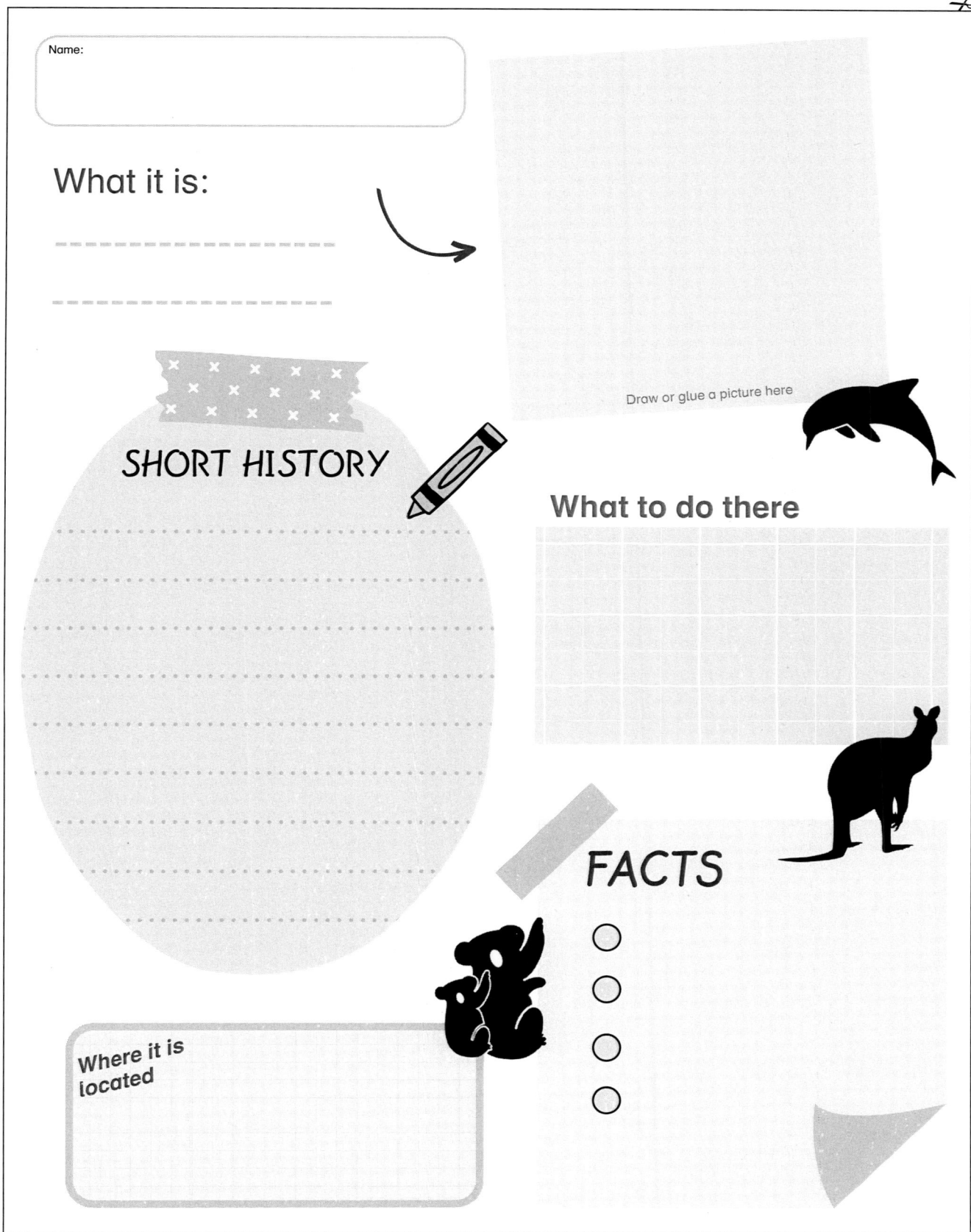

Name:

What it is:

Draw or glue a picture here

SHORT HISTORY

What to do there

FACTS

Where it is located

Australian animals

▶ Cut out the pictures and glue them on the right part of the leparello. Do you know the names of these special animals? Write them on the leparello.

▶ Cut out the two parts of the leparello, glue it, fold it and fix it on your lapbook.

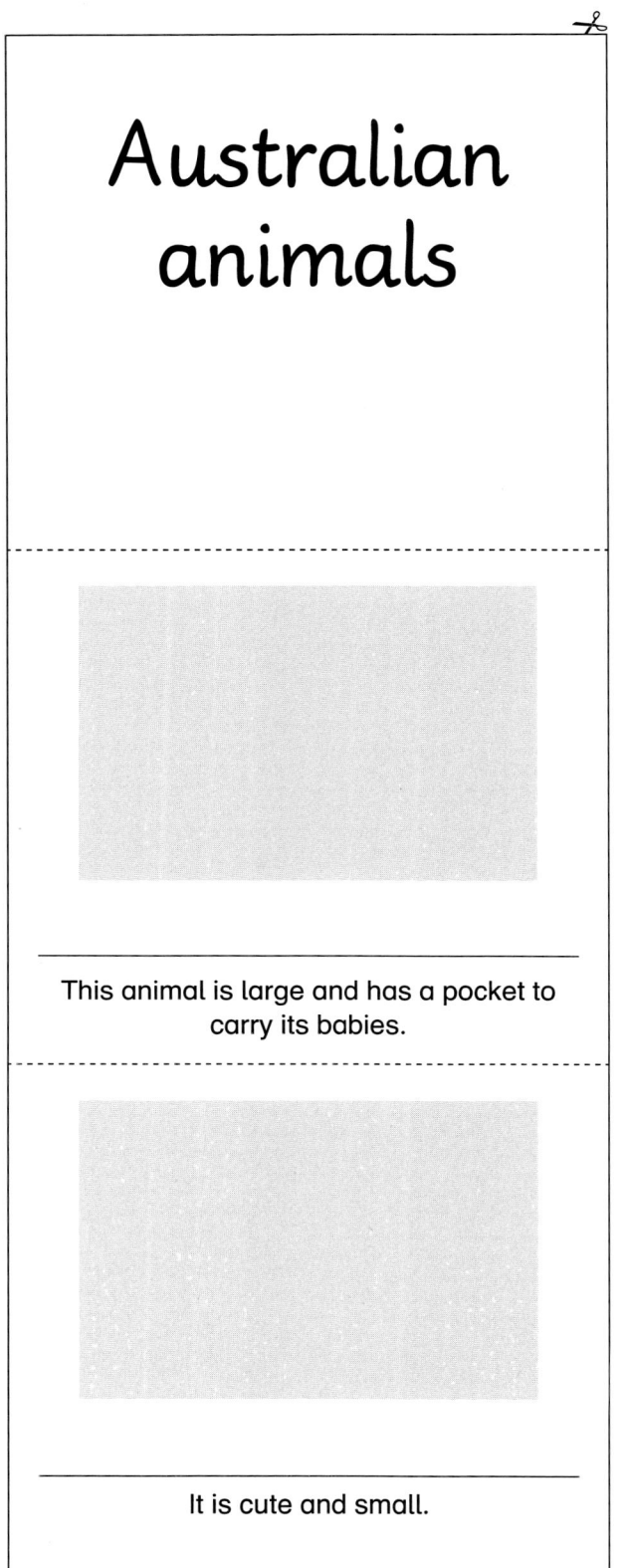

Australian animals

This animal is large and has a pocket to carry its babies.

It is cute and small.

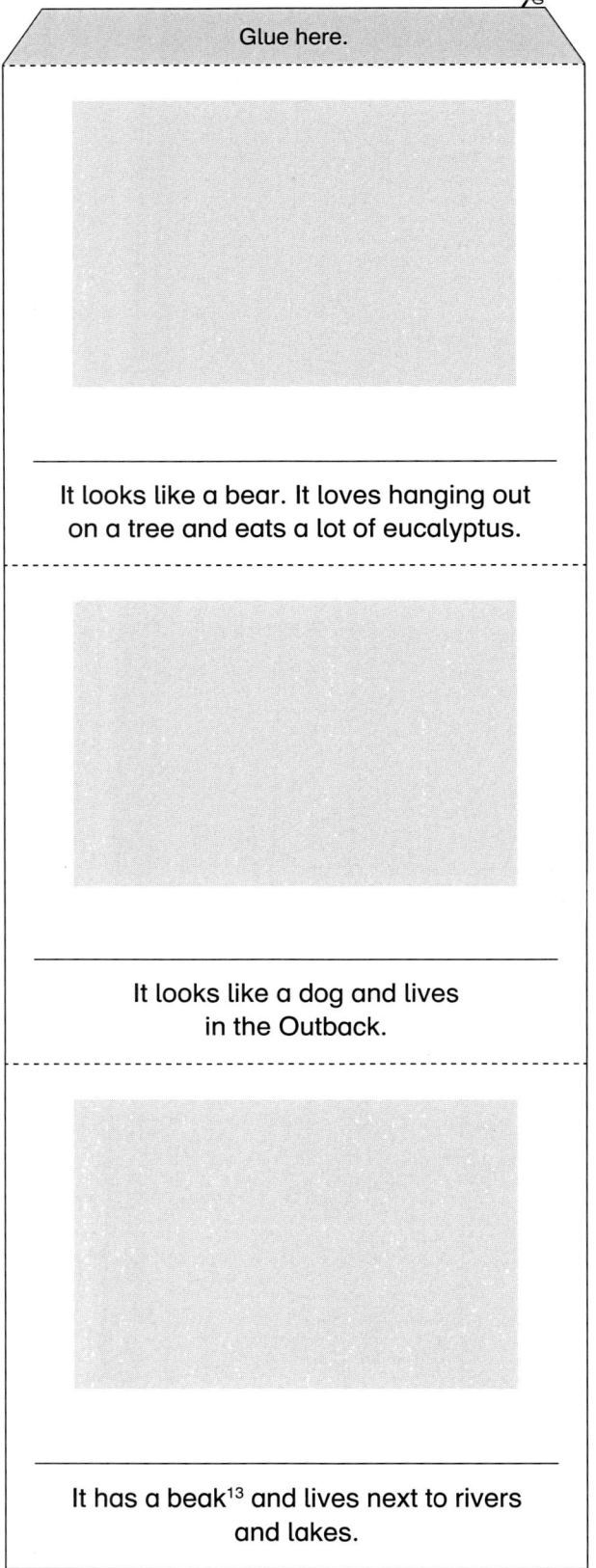

Glue here.

It looks like a bear. It loves hanging out on a tree and eats a lot of eucalyptus.

It looks like a dog and lives in the Outback.

It has a beak[13] and lives next to rivers and lakes.

[13] beak = *Schnabel*

Greetings from Australia

▶ You are on a holiday in Australia and want to tell your family and friends about the landscape, sights and life in Australia. Choose between task a) writing a postcard or task b) writing a text message. What did you like the most and why?

a) A postcard from Australia

▶ You can design the front of your postcard on your own. Cut it out and glue it on your lapbook!

Glue here.

b) A text message from Australia

▶ Answer the questions from your friend! Cut out the illustration and glue it on your lapbook!

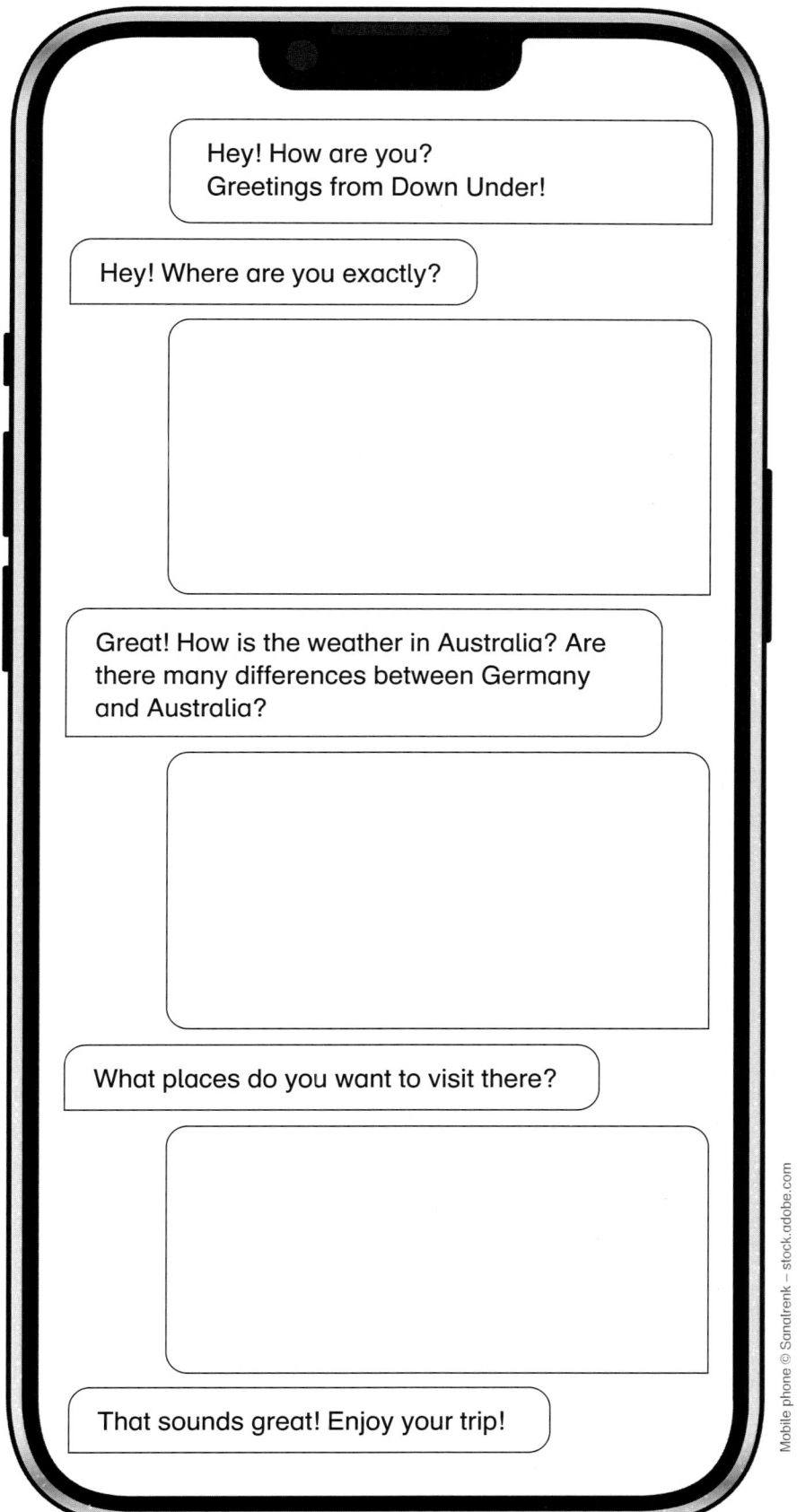

Hey! How are you?
Greetings from Down Under!

Hey! Where are you exactly?

Great! How is the weather in Australia? Are there many differences between Germany and Australia?

What places do you want to visit there?

That sounds great! Enjoy your trip!

Mobile phone © Sanatrenk — stock.adobe.com